Praise for *Guru, Inc.*

"The creator economy isn't the future; it's the present. Millions are posting every day, but very few know how to actually turn attention into a brand and a business. This book is the road map creators have been waiting for."

—Daniel Mac (@ItsDanielMac),
Social Media Influencer, "What do you do for a living?"

"I've spent my career in traditional media, watching how television and magazines shaped culture and built icons. But today, the center of gravity has shifted. Social media is everything. AJ and his team helped me capitalize on it, and they're brilliant. Read AJ's book."

—Nikki Haskell (@BigNikBH), Grandfluencer,
Television Host, Entrepreneur, and Media Pioneer

"If you have a mission in your heart, you can't keep it hidden. Social media is one of the most powerful ways to communicate that mission, win attention, and change lives. That's what AJ teaches in this book. He cares deeply, and he'll guide you to share your message with the world in a way that inspires and impacts. Read his book! It's your playbook for making your mission matter."

—Warren Phillips (@NonToxicDad),
Wellness Educator, Author, Speaker, and Scientist

"*Guru, Inc.* is a master class in how to break through the noise, tell your story, and not just go viral—but create lasting impact. As someone who has learned the power of owning my message, my category, and broadening my reach to a global audience, AJ's lessons on positioning and service have been transformative. His framework of owning your category early and serving audiences instead of selling them is something he's taught me personally—and that I've watched him teach countless others. This book will help you not only master those techniques but also shape a message that resonates far beyond yourself. It's a masterful road map that dismantles shadow beliefs about worth and unlocks the truth that your potential is limitless."

—Kudzi Chikumbu (@SirCandleMan), Fragrance and Lifestyle
Content Creator, Media Executive, Author, and Speaker

"Every great company is built on a leader's vision. True success comes when that vision is communicated with clarity and energy to everyone who matters, inside and outside the business. AJ's book shows you how to master that art in today's fast-moving social media world. *Guru, Inc.* provides the insight and tools to share your vision with confidence and impact."

—Roy Cammarano, Business Strategist and
Author, *Entrepreneurial Transitions*

"In today's virtual world, it's not enough to just be a professional on the surface. You need real expertise, intuitive insight, and the ability to make that visible to the world. Whether you're a real estate agent, a small business owner, or a CEO, AJ shows you how to do exactly that and position yourself where it matters most."

—Neil Schwartz, Founder, Century 21 Masters

GURU, INC.

GURU, INC.

Win in the Creator Economy,
Build an Iconic Brand, and Become
the Go-To Authority in Your Niche

AJ KUMAR

MATT
HOLT

Matt Holt Books
An Imprint of BenBella Books, Inc.
Dallas, TX

Matt Holt is an imprint of BenBella Books, Inc.
8080 N. Central Expressway
Suite 1700
Dallas, TX 75206
benbellabooks.com
Send feedback to feedback@benbellabooks.com

Matt Holt and *BenBella* are federally registered trademarks.

Printed in the United States of America
10 9 8 7 6 5 4 3 2 1

Library of Congress Control Number: 2025036184
ISBN 9781637748442 (hardcover)
ISBN 9781637748459 (electronic)

Editing by Lydia Choi
Copyediting by Evan Herrington
Proofreading by Lisa Story and Ashley Casteel
Text design and composition by PerfecType, Nashville, TN
Cover design by Brigid Pearson
Cover image © Adobe Stock / MicroOne

Special discounts for bulk sales are available. Please contact bulkorders@benbellabooks.com.

To the part of you that sees yourself in me. This book is a mirror. You're not just remembering me. You're remembering who you are.

CONTENTS

Foreword by Neil Patel   xi

Introduction: A New Awakening   1

A Note from the Author   9

1. The Guru Effect   13

2. A Tomato Is a Fruit   23

3. Spiritual Gurus vs. Business Gurus   35

4. From Homes to Home Pages   43

5. Perception Over Talent   55

6. The Celebrity Guru Phenomenon   65

7. Building Your Personal Guru Brand   75

8. The Guru Ladder   89

9. Attention Economics   107

10. Return on Attention Created   119

11. The Hidden Language of Virality   131

12. Adapt Like a Digital Native   149

13. The Personal Media Company Model   159

14. Breaking the VOLT   175

15. The Guru's Journey 185

16. "Darketing" 201

17. The Power of Selflessness: Serving Your Audience 215

18. Embracing the Guru Within: Awakening the Power
in You 223

Afterword: The Final Awakening 229

Acknowledgments 233

Notes 235

FOREWORD

In a world where everyone fights for attention, only a few rise to the top and stay there. What sets them apart? It's not luck. It's a strategy. And this book will show you how it is done.

As the cofounder of NP Digital, a global advertising agency, I've helped some of the world's biggest brands navigate the complexities of online marketing. I've built one of the most recognized personal brands in the marketing industry, and through that journey, I've seen firsthand how the Creator Economy has transformed the business landscape.

I've known AJ Kumar since high school, and from day one, I knew he was wired differently. He's not just a marketer or a strategist. He's someone who has spent years behind the scenes helping subject-matter experts. His focus? Turning their knowledge into real online businesses that attract attention and drive revenue. From wellness coaches to real estate trainers to TV personalities, he's helped them go from overlooked to in demand. This book distills those lessons for anyone looking to become the go-to authority in their niche.

Guru, Inc. isn't just about growing a following. It's about understanding how attention really works in the Creator Economy so you can build a personal brand that drives real business results. You'll learn how to turn fleeting views into loyal communities and how to monetize your expertise without chasing trends.

Inside these pages, AJ shares powerful frameworks like the Guru Ladder and introduces concepts such as attention as a currency—something you can use, invest, and direct to build connection, trust, and revenue. You'll get step-by-step guidance on how to position yourself, create valuable content, and build a thriving business around your brand.

I've seen this firsthand. I helped AJ launch his first blog, watched him cofound a marketing agency, and later saw him pivot to focus entirely on personal brands. I remember one night when he called me, excited about helping a celebrity nutritionist build her online presence. At the time, it sounded like a long shot. Personal brands weren't booming yet, and success stories in niche industries were rare. But AJ saw what others missed: the rise of the Creator Economy and how it would transform the way people build brands and businesses.

And he was right. AJ helped that nutritionist build a thriving business with millions of website visitors and a devoted community that followed her every word. AJ took the same principles and replicated the success across different industries—real estate coaches, reality TV stars, and health experts. He helped them not only grow their audiences but also turn their expertise into real businesses.

This book breaks down the systems behind how experts become household names in the Creator Economy. You'll learn how to turn attention into real business results by transforming curiosity into trust, and trust into long-term influence. Attention, like currency, has value, and when you focus it in the right places, it creates connection, credibility, and growth. With clear, actionable steps, you will learn how to position yourself, craft content that resonates, and build a personal brand people remember and respect.

At my agency, NP Digital, we see this shift every day. Global brands are shifting their budgets toward content creators who foster genuine audience relationships. Traditional advertising is evolving, with more focus on authentic, story-driven content from trusted experts and educators. People don't want slogans. They want connection. They don't want ads. They want insight from someone they trust. AJ saw this shift early and has been helping experts turn their knowledge into influence that drives real transformation.

The strategies you'll find here aren't based on theory. They come from real-world experience, hard-won insights, and a relentless commitment to understanding what makes people pay attention, care, and take action.

The world doesn't reward noise. It rewards clarity, connection, and consistency. If you're ready to break through the noise and position yourself as the go-to authority in your niche, turn the page. The strategies are here. Now, it is your move.

Neil Patel
Cofounder of NP Digital and *New York Times* bestselling author

INTRODUCTION
A New Awakening

What if life is just a dream, and when you die, you wake up?

My grandpa, with his thick Punjabi accent, had ambitiously posed the philosophical question to me, a 10-year-old AJ Kumar, while on one of our Sunday family road trips. Even as a child, I always enjoyed solving problems and allowing my mind to wander in all sorts of curious directions. I remember sitting silently in the back seat of the Kumar family's burgundy Toyota Previa minivan, staring out of the half-opened window.

What if life is just a dream, and when you die, you wake up?

This question is the cornerstone of how I think about life and business. It was the spark that ignited my own personal awakening. And hopefully, by the time you finish reading this book, it can do the same for you. Each day, when we rise to start our morning routines, we are waking up to a brand-new reality. Most of us probably don't ever pause to think about it that way, but the truth is, each of us only has so many days on this planet. We can waste them, or we can use them to create and enjoy the life we want to live.

As a young boy, I tried to tackle that question for the duration of the car ride. I continued to think about it all the way home too. I thought about it in bed that night. And I even thought about it this morning while eating breakfast as a 36-year-old digital marketing professional. I thought about it because the question had planted the seed in my mind that ultimately led me, some decades later, to having a power that's as pretty darn close as it gets to magic. My career is to help people *wake up* to their unique, limitless potential.

The conclusions that I've drawn from that simple-sounding question are deserving of an entire book of its own, but my core conclusion is this: Most people are living someone else's dream. They are following scripts written by their parents, teachers, or society about what success should look like. But the digital world has changed everything. For the first time in history, you don't need permission to build your own stage or create your own version of success.

In my years building digital brands for founders, CEOs, and a variety of subject matter experts, I've seen what separates those who get noticed from those who get ignored. I've scaled a celebrity nutritionist's expertise into a multimillion-dollar business, transformed an 84-year-old forgotten socialite into a viral sensation with millions of monthly views, and guided a creator who now reaches 30 million monthly viewers while helping families across the globe make healthier choices.

But even among the most driven and accomplished people I've worked with, one surprising pattern kept showing up: They couldn't stand social media. They viewed it like an entry-level position that they could just off-load onto their college-aged niece or nephew. Or, they believed that if they posted on social media consistently for a few weeks, the algorithm would magically just take care of the rest. Rather than get behind the wheel and drive themselves toward their dreams, they sat passively in the passenger seat and were disappointed when they couldn't reproduce the jaw-dropping viral results they'd seen their colleagues and competitors create. Part of what's to blame for their naivety is that we've all been conditioned to play *the old media game.*

Before social media gave everyone the power of a Hollywood studio in their pocket, the old game was the only game in town. You know all about the old game, even if you don't realize you do. Chances are, you've been secretly taught to play it your whole life. Celebrity authorities like Oprah, Ellen, and Martha Stewart mastered the traditional media game because they knew the secrets to generating attention at scale, which I'll be teaching you in this book.

The old media dream was sold to the masses, right in front of their very eyes, without them ever even noticing. Nearly every billboard, every window display, and every television commercial promises you the toxic silver lining hidden behind the old media dream: the chance to be a star. They promoted the idea that this was an equal opportunity, freely available to everyone.

But what they didn't tell you is that only a handful of people were actually lucky enough to achieve this dream. That's just how the system worked. If you wanted a shot, you needed a Hollywood agent, a major decision-maker, or a person with connections to get you in the room. It was passive, controlled, and built to keep the power in someone else's hands. You had no real power to shape your future or claim ownership of the life you were meant to create. This meant most people were playing the game like spectators. Idly sitting by watching television while silently hoping and praying that one day a network executive would pick up a golden telephone, thumb through their Rolodex, and pull up *your* name—like a winning lottery ticket number. Maybe then you'd get the call and a chance to be on TV. And just like that . . . *poof!* Your life would magically change overnight.

It's no secret that this pipe dream never materialized for the masses. It was a shiny veneer that made a few select elites very wealthy, and it was gatekept for a reason. In this model, your role was to *consume*, not to *create*. You were conditioned to watch other people living the life of your dreams so that you would continue to buy the latest and greatest shiny new object, tune into the hottest prime-time reality show, or buy the latest best-selling book hot off the shelves. Despite their promise of making you better, giving you success, and getting you rich, what they really sold you was an illusory goal that left you feeling empty and hungry for more. To them, it was all about signaling a dream—a signpost bigger than the Hollywood sign—that very few were lucky enough to live for themselves. You couldn't create your way to the top; you had to be chosen.

But then social media came along like a giant bulldozer and leveled the playing field. Now, there was a new game in town, and the only gatekeeper was the startup capital required to buy a smartphone and a data plan, for around 100 bucks per month. Seemingly overnight, you no longer had to be cast on a major network television show to be seen, heard, and taken seriously at scale. Today, you no longer need a studio. You *are* the studio. You no longer need a network executive to give you permission. You *are* the network.

You don't need to wait weeks to get your content greenlit like you did in the old days. If you want to create something, you push a few buttons and upload it to social media, where it has the potential to reach millions of eyeballs. For the first time in recorded human history, everyone has the chance to live their dreams online. In the words of Walt Disney: "If you can dream it, you can do it."

So how do you realize this expansive, limitless potential for yourself? First, you need to recognize that social media is a game. And like any good game, it's meant to challenge you, stretch your imagination, and reward those who learn how to play it well. The real shift isn't in how hard you work. It's in who you're working for. This time, you're not climbing someone else's ladder—you're building your own. For most people who view social media as a passive chore, the alarm clock hasn't gone off for them yet, and they are still stuck dreaming about the promises of the old media sales pitch. Instead, you need to recondition yourself to start thinking like a creator—someone who has the tools and experience to master the game for themselves. But you can't win a game if you don't even know you're playing one. You also can't improve your performance unless you understand the rules of the game and how it works.

It's not always easy. Just because it's a game doesn't mean it isn't hard. Any game worth playing has its own set of challenges. But being aware of them makes it so much easier. And that's where I come in. As the *digital maestro*, I help you understand how to win this game. Just like the hours I spent as a kid sitting around the kitchen table with my family playing the board game The Game of Life, growing your audience, brand, and business today requires paying attention to how the game is designed. And on social media, that design is intentional. Every major platform is built on a gamification system that keeps people hooked. But once you understand the structure, it becomes easier to navigate. At its core, every game, whether it's social media, chess, or football, can be broken down into three simple elements: goals, blocks, and moves. Master those, and you move from passive spectator on the sidelines to an active player on the field.

The *goals* of the game represent what you are trying to accomplish by playing. For most of you, that means establishing yourself as the go-to authority in your space, growing a business with real impact, and using your platform to positively influence the people who watch you.

The *blocks* are the challenges that stand in your way. This is ironically what makes playing any game meaningful, exciting, and even a little addictive. Think of one of the most basic games on the planet: *Tetris*. If you didn't have blocks or challenges, as annoying as they can be, you wouldn't want to play the game. It would be the real-life equivalent of playing on "god mode." If everyone got millions of views every time they posted, the value would diminish, and it would get boring after a while.

The *moves* represent the strategic moves you need to make so that you can overcome the blocks and reach your goals. On social media, that means choosing the right hooks, formats, and topics—the building blocks of content that actually gets noticed. It's the way you show up, what you say, how you say it, and how you structure your message so that people stop scrolling and start paying attention. Today, the new media game isn't about being chosen—it's about choosing yourself.

You see, in the age of AI-powered content, personal brands are actually going to be *more* vital than ever before. People will crave human-centric content that is rich in personality and authenticity. These facets make people want to engage with your content. Your end goal is to have people remember your name, image, and likeness—what I call building your Personal Media Company (which I'll explain in detail later). This is where you build a business around a recognizable identity, earn deep trust, and gain real leverage. Because in this new era, while algorithms surface content based on interests and engagement patterns, people ultimately choose to trust and follow the creators behind that content. Social media users don't just consume information; they connect with the people who consistently deliver value in their areas of expertise. The irony is that traditional old media stars are trying to get into new media. The lines are beginning to blur, and as the rules of the game begin to change and transform, people will be looking for someone they can trust.

In this book, I'm unveiling my vision for the future. In the days to come, it won't be influencers who look pretty or experts who sound smart who rise to the top. It will be those who speak with conviction, passion, and wisdom. People who combine deep expertise with genuine care for helping others. In my Indian heritage, we called these people gurus. Leaders whose words carried weight not because they were loud, but because they were rooted in clarity, experience, and truth.

Every generation has an opportunity in front of them. My grandfather couldn't have ever dreamed of the opportunities available to me today. This is the dream he was speaking about that I woke up to, and my hope for you is that by the time you finish reading this book, you'll wake up to your dream as well.

I've spent the last 20 years working alongside modern-day gurus—the go-to authorities in their niches who appear on TV, get interviewed by top media publications, and influence millions of people around the world. I've watched them rise, studied their methods, and learned what separates those who simply seek fame from those who generate real impact. What I've discovered is that the modern guru isn't defined by credentials or the number of social media followers. They're defined by something much harder to replicate: lived experience.

In an age where AI can mimic almost everything—the production quality, the perfect lighting, even the way someone speaks—there's one thing it can't fake: the trust that comes from having actually walked the path you're teaching others to follow. The only content creators I see who will be impossible to replicate are those sharing their genuine human experience, because the moment you lose that authenticity, you lose everything that matters.

Today's leading experts understand that people don't just want information, they want transformation. They've seen the terrain, walked it themselves, and now light the path for others. Their authority isn't based on hype or perfect content, it's based on resonance. They offer more than advice; they offer proof that change is possible, because they've lived it.

The question my grandfather asked me all those years ago wasn't just about death and dreams. It was about awakening to the reality that you have the power to create the life you want to live. And in this new game, that power isn't theoretical; it's practical, immediate, and available to anyone willing to step up and claim it.

Guru, Inc. is your roadmap to joining the ranks of those who don't just play the game but also change it. The field is level. The tools are in your hands. And the only person standing between you and the life you're meant to create is the version of yourself that's still waiting for permission. It's time to wake up from the dream you inherited and start building the one that's truly yours.

A NOTE FROM THE AUTHOR

WELCOME TO GURU, INC.

Throughout the course of this book, I'll pull back the curtains on personal stories from my business journey, as well as anecdotes from clients and celebrities who fit the guru mold. The early chapters will focus on stories about entrepreneurship, while the second half of the book focuses on the models, systems, and terminology that can help you attain guru status for yourself.

But before we go any further, you're probably wondering, *AJ, what exactly is a guru?*

I have no doubt that you are familiar with the general concept of a guru—a wise person, a teacher, a leader, a smarter-than-everyone-else-er. It's a well-used word in the Western world, especially these days. And beyond its original and traditional definition, it's a word commonly borrowed by just about every industry. Management guru, yoga guru, fitness guru, psychology guru, search engine optimization (SEO) guru, science guru, low-carb vegan diet guru . . . the list is seemingly endless. But the concept of a "guru" originates from my culture. It's a very Indian thing, and it's a core element in the traditions of Indian culture. So let's start with a few definitions.

Over the past decade, I've watched a major cultural shift unfold. The old dream was to be a celebrity, walk the red carpet, star in movies, and be adored by millions. Then came the influencer wave: everyday people chasing followers, brand deals, and algorithm fame. But something shifted. The term "influencer" became watered down with more noise and less meaning. In response, a new identity started rising in its place: the thought leader. No longer satisfied with just being liked or followed, the next generation of experts and entrepreneurs wanted to be respected. They wanted their ideas to matter. They didn't just want fame; they wanted influence.

An influencer is a creator with a large following that can impact their audience's purchasing behaviors. They are an expert at leveraging attention, but they lack the depth of expertise to help their followers truly transform. A thought leader, on the other hand, is someone recognized as an authoritative voice within a chosen field, someone who has the power to shape discourse, disrupt industry best practices, and influence how others think about their chosen niche.

But what about those thought leaders who seem to always command respect, whose products and services are heralded as innovative, legendary, and even life-changing? This upper echelon of expertise is the sacred territory that is reserved only for *gurus*.

A guru is what I challenge all my clients to aspire to be, because it is the absolute highest version of themselves—where passion meets incredible influence. A *guru* is a next-level thought leader whose impact on the world has transcended mere expertise. They've developed a proprietary framework that has attracted a devoted and impassioned following. Gurus do more than simply inform; they *transform* their audience's understanding of themselves to help them get results that they never thought were possible.

Where experts, coaches, and consultants are transactional, selling their knowledge, services, or content for money, gurus are the opposite.

They unleash their transformative power to launch movements, shift public perceptions, and change lives. They do more than just deliver groundbreaking information; they reframe how people think, act, and lead. Gurus inspire change that sweeps across entire industries, inspiring everyone who comes into contact with their knowledge.

As a concept, the title *Guru, Inc.* is the marriage of two unique concepts: becoming a guru who is highly sought after for their expertise, and creating a business model that transforms that expertise into the creation of a "new" media empire. In the digital age, attention is currency, and those who position themselves as gurus have the most leverage, opportunity, and wealth-building potential. The amazing part about the digital landscape is that anyone can transform into a guru by adopting a new mindset and following a proven framework.

Throughout this book, when I refer to "experts," I'm talking about you, the reader with knowledge to share. When I say "content creators," I'm referring to the broader landscape of people making content on social media. My goal is to help you stand out in that crowded space by leveraging your unique expertise.

This book is about mastering the transition from expert to go-to authority. It's a playbook for turning your hard-earned expertise into a powerful, modern presence that moves people to act, share, and remember, not just consume.

Let's be clear: Being an expert in your field and building a personal brand are two different skill sets. You might be exceptional at what you do, but unless you know how to communicate that value in the right formats, your expertise won't reach the people who need it. This isn't about becoming a full-time content creator. It's about learning how to market yourself effectively, using the platforms and tools where attention lives now—social platforms, search results, and mobile apps.

In the past, that attention lived on TV or in traditional media. Today, it lives in TikTok clips, YouTube videos, Reels, podcasts, and carousel posts. If you want to lead in the digital age, you need to master the skill of making your expertise seen, heard, and felt—in the language your audience already speaks. This book will teach you how to build that system, from the inside out. Not with surface-level tricks, but with the strategy, psychology, and positioning to make your expertise truly resonate in the digital age.

The idea for this book came as a natural result of observing this evolution in real time with my clients who have gone on to build seven- and eight-figure guru businesses for themselves. I've witnessed firsthand how people (from social media influencers to business icons) have built authority and monetized their personal brands. I've recognized that in the modern world, a guru isn't necessarily the wisest or most enlightened person—it's someone who has mastered attention, perception, and influence. My goal in the following pages is to map out the exact steps you can take to thrive in the Creator Economy—where expertise, storytelling, and positioning rather than just raw knowledge and traditional credentials determine success. Becoming a guru is a process, not an accident. Allow me to guide you on this incredible journey.

Once again, welcome to *Guru, Inc.* I'm glad you're here.

Chapter 1
THE GURU EFFECT

I spent my childhood years growing up in Cyprus ...

Maybe you are picturing an exotic island in the Mediterranean Sea. Or a mental image of giant palm trees, or the delicious thought of Halloumi cheese. Perhaps you're anticipating the promise of a romantic story that such an opening sentence surely hints at. *Ah*, you might think, *I saw the author's photo on the back cover, and I just knew he looked like a foreigner! Now it makes sense!*

But in the pursuit of full disclosure, I have to add an extra two words for clarity: I spent my childhood years growing up in Cypress, *Southern California*. The exotic-intrigue-o-meter dial just swung left (sorry). But nevertheless, my childhood did indeed have elements of foreign and ancient culture. So, I won't let you down!

THE MOST VALUABLE TOOL IN THE UNIVERSE

I was a second-generation Indian immigrant kid in an all-American town. With a single suitcase and a dream, my grandpa left India in the 1970s to set up a new life in the Great US of A (Oakland, California, to be geographically specific). I imagine how difficult that journey must have been—how difficult a decision it must have been to leave the safety and familiarity of a small Indian village, to arrive empty-handed and without marketable skills in a totally foreign, fast-paced, "big city, bright lights" country. But he was far from being original. Nearly five million immigrants arrived in the United States during the 1970s, the greatest influx of people to America since the 1920s.

Such large numbers of immigrants do not happen by coincidence. There was something that drew so many to America. Challenging and ambitious journeys are almost always motivated by one specific thing. It's the reason that motivated Sam and Frodo to journey 1,350 miles (barefoot) through Middle Earth; it's the reason why every year over 1.5 million wildebeests walk 500 miles through Tanzania; it's the reason why those two Scottish guys from the Proclaimers explained in the chorus of their '80s hit song that they were perfectly willing to walk 500 miles (and were, in fact, open to the idea of walking 500 more). So, what is this specific and magical reason? It's something that America sells better than any other nation on Earth . . .

It's hope.

A GURU IN THE FAMILY

OK, we got a little sidetracked from the opening sentence, so let's circle back to it: I was a second-generation Indian immigrant kid in an all-American town. I was fortunate to grow up in a home that straddled two rich cultures. In many ways, I grew up as a typical American kid. But my life was also filled with the traditions, stories, and values (and food) of my Indian heritage. While my parents tirelessly worked through the day and night, I was, for the most part, raised by my grandma. She only spoke Punjabi. On Saturday mornings, I'd watch the adventures of the *Mighty Morphin Power Rangers* and learn vocabulary from *Ninja*

Turtles ("Cowabunga!" for example). But I'd also listen to the tales of the Hindu god Krishna, and my grandpa got me totally hooked on watching *Mahabharat*—a TV show about ancient Indian stories. Nothing excited a 10-year-old AJ more than watching an episode on the escapades of the mighty (and completely mischievous) monkey god Hanuman ji.

In the literal sense, I grew up in a family of six:

1. Mom
2. Dad
3. Grandpa
4. Grandma
5. Little brother, Jason
6. The Wonderful and Charismatic AJ

But I always felt that we were, in fact, a family of seven. Our home had the constant presence of another family figure. His name was Baba Ji. He was always in our home. Each of us in the family had our own unique and special connection to him. He was, in some way, the head of the Kumar household. He had an answer to any question we might have about life. He inspired us, and knowing that we could rely on him brought a sense of calm to our lives. We greeted him every day, though he never once opened his mouth to speak back. He wore the same thing all the time—a crème-colored turban and a matching outfit. He had a lengthy white beard, which made him stick out like a sore thumb. His face had a pleasant and open expression that never wavered, and the gentle gaze of his eyes was one of love, acceptance, and wisdom.

Baba Ji was not like any other human you would know. And that's not because he never spoke to us—or changed his clothes or facial expression. Those characteristics only sound unusual because they are out of context. Baba Ji was in the form of an 18" × 24" poster within a neat basswood frame.

Baba Ji was a guru.

But more importantly, Baba Ji was *our* guru.

MY FIRST GURU EXPERIENCE

Baba Ji straddled two worlds. In our minds and hearts, he held the place of an almost mythical godlike being. But, at the same time, he was very much a real, living, breathing human being.

Every so often, a guru would come to our town (or at least relatively close by), and these moments were overwhelmingly exciting highlights of my childhood. A few weeks or months before their arrival, the rumors would start. There'd be chatter in the community about someone who knew someone who heard from someone else that "guru X" was coming to visit and give a talk. Word would spread quickly, and when it was officially confirmed, the excitement in the community was almost feverish.

Thousands upon thousands of people would make their travel plans and clear their schedules to attend the *satsang*. A *satsang* is a public gathering where a guru speaks and answers questions. The word is derived from the root *sat*, which in ancient Sanskrit means "purity" or "truth." Throughout the years, there were numerous occasions where I found myself squeezed in the back seat along with my brother, Jason, and my grandparents in the family's magenta Toyota Previa, headed for a *satsang* in Palm Springs. On one of these occasions, we were headed to attend a *satsang*, where our guru, Baba Ji, was to be speaking!

I was around 10 years old when I attended Baba Ji's *satsang*. That was almost three decades ago, but still, to this day, I remember every little detail of it with remarkable clarity. I certainly didn't realize it at the time, but that experience was my first real education on the topic on which I would, decades later, base my professional career. The insights that the experience gave 10-year-old AJ were the seeds from which I later developed my philosophy and approach to digital marketing and building multimillion-dollar brands.

These are the four key insights that Baba Ji's *satsang* taught me about the immense and unique power and influence of a guru. Some were clear to me as a child, and some I realized as an adult looking back at the experience. But all of them left an indelible, lasting impression on me. In fact, they inspired me to write this book.

1. **A guru does not need a marketing budget—a guru gains new followers organically.** Thousands of people attended Baba Ji's *satsang*. But leading up to the event, there was hardly any marketing or advertising. Organic, word-of-mouth promotion was all he needed. Without anything else, news of his event still spread like wildfire because *a guru commands attention*.

2. **A guru is prioritized over everything.** When your usual event comes to town, people typically consider a number of things before deciding whether to get tickets. But when you get the rare and magical opportunity to attend a guru's event, the logistics don't matter—you can strap the kids on top of the minivan if need be. The whole family is going! Everything else can wait.

3. **A guru alone is the entire experience.** A guru is certainly a category of celebrity. What is unique about a guru, versus most other kinds of performances or events, is that the entire experience is simply the guru themselves, seated on a stage with a microphone. There is no need for anything else—no pyrotechnics, no big sound system, no flashing lights or professional dancers or backup singers or surprise cameo appearances. The audience wants one thing only: the guru.

4. **A guru's advice is sacred, and that's why it is life-changing.** A guru has a rare position in society. With the title of "guru," they have the very highest level of respect from their audience. They have already earned the respect of their followers, and therefore whatever they say, whatever answer or piece of advice they give, whatever stories they tell—their words are considered sacred and accepted as truth and wisdom without question. The guru is always right.

These points make the status of having the "guru" title an incredibly powerful and unique position. A guru has a power that is unlike any other member of society. As a child, that absolutely fascinated me. The idea of a guru was in many ways similar to the superheroes that I watched on TV. But they actually existed in the real world!

THE WAYS OF THE GURU

As children, we idolize superheroes. We all have our favorites (mine was the guy in the red suit from *Mighty Morphin Power Rangers*). Every superhero has special powers. A superhero résumé would seem odd without at least one, right? Superman can travel faster than a speeding bullet. Spider-Man can shoot usefully sticky webs from his wrists and swing between buildings. Batman has tons of money and a super cool car.

So, what was Baba Ji's superpower?

It's not something that can really be explained in a few words. So, I'll explain it by telling you the story of my experience.

I guess I wasn't quite sure what to expect him to be like. To me, he was in the "superhero" category. But he was in the "god" category too. I had never seen such a person in real life. It was exciting, but there was also a bit of fear. On the long drive to the *satsang* in Palm Springs (thankfully, this time I had sprinted to the car ahead of my brother and claimed the window seat), I stared out the window and imagined what it was going to be like in his presence. Would he, like a mighty god, have a loud and deep, booming voice that filled the auditorium? Would he be surrounded by a heavenly spiritual glow? What if he saw me in the audience and judged me? He knew everything, and maybe that meant he could read my mind. *Maybe I'm not really worthy of being in his presence*, I wondered. *I'm only a pretty insignificant 10-year-old after all . . .*

I, along with the whole Kumar family, was lucky to get pretty good seats. We were probably about 10 or so rows from the stage. The stage was empty except for two chairs. A smartly dressed man walked on stage, and the audience of thousands fell deathly silent. It was that "you could hear a pin drop" kind of silence. The man welcomed everyone and rattled off a list of thank-yous to the event organizers, sponsors, and people who helped put the *satsang* together. He then enthusiastically announced that Baba Ji was ready and welcomed him to the stage.

I literally held my breath.

Baba Ji appeared. He was wearing a crème-colored tunic and white turban, just like in our framed poster at home! And his long white beard was just as I'd pictured it. He put his hands together humbly in thanks, gave a small bow to the crowd, and took his seat.

When Baba Ji took the microphone and started speaking, I was taken by complete surprise. He was so normal. He was just like a regular guy! In fact, he was a really nice guy! His voice was calm and friendly, and he smiled warmly between sentences. The way he spoke, the way he sat in his chair, the words that he used, the tone of his voice . . . it all just struck me as being incredibly humble and genuine. There was no ego. He was not a showman putting on a spectacular performance to dazzle and impress.

Over the next two hours or so, Baba Ji continued to speak. He answered questions from the interviewer onstage and took many questions from people in the audience as well. He told stories, gave words of wisdom, and every now and then made us all laugh.

In the eyes of a 10-year-old AJ Kumar, these are the five "superpowers" that I realized Baba Ji had. These are the things that gave him the status of guru:

1. **Personal connection.** When Baba Ji spoke, I felt like he was speaking to me. I was seated in a hall with thousands of people. I was no one special. I wasn't even an adult. But I didn't feel like an outsider. When he spoke, it felt intimate and personal. After

that evening, I felt like I had met him and spent time with him. Still to this day, I remember our "time together" fondly.

2. **Personal relatability.** The audience was made up of a wide spectrum of society. There were people of all different ages, education levels, professions, and financial situations. Baba Ji had a way of talking and explaining things that everyone in the audience could not only understand but personally relate to.

3. **Empathy and understanding.** When Baba Ji answered the many questions from the audience, I was amazed at how much he understood about the everyday lives of normal people. I had suspected that someone that lived life as a guru did not experience the world like us. Surely Baba Ji, with all his wisdom, power, and influence, wouldn't have had to struggle with "normal" challenges. I couldn't imagine a great and mighty guru wrestling with things like being poor or depressed, or doubting his faith, or trying to quit smoking, or having to navigate a difficult relationship with an overbearing mother-in-law. But when Baba Ji was asked about these things, he humbly answered in a way that revealed how he had, in many ways, experienced normal everyday life, just like everyone in the audience. He revealed his humanity. It made everyone feel so much better about themselves. Even the great guru had to face the same problems that we do!

4. **Generosity.** Although the guru's thousands of followers would have been satisfied to hear just a few wise sentences, Baba Ji was exceptionally generous with his time and attention. Even though a guru must spend their life being surrounded by endless people wanting their attention and advice—a grueling traveling schedule to attend *satsangs* just like this one all around the world, months upon months of hard work writing his books, and on top of all that, a need for an incredible amount of time spent in

solitude reading, researching, and meditating (the actual core ingredient of his guru-ness)—Baba Ji was calm, patient, and fully present. Whenever a question was asked, he never gave one-sentence answers. Whether the question was as complex as "Why is there so much suffering in the world?" or as (seemingly) simple as "How often should I meditate?" Baba Ji would consider each with the same respect and worthiness of his deepest thoughts and attention. After each question was asked, he would nod his head in a way that, without words, showed that he understood and respected the question. Before he spoke to give his answer, he would take a brief silent pause to think. His answers did not come across as rehearsed. They were from the heart, and Baba Ji took as much time as was needed to give the best answer he could.

5. **Entertainment and education.** A *satsang* is ultimately an event about education. A guru is, at the end of the day, a teacher, and the audience are pupils learning lessons. I was in fifth grade, and I knew all about sitting through lessons. Even school subjects that I enjoyed, like math, were tiring about halfway through the class. My mind would start to wander, and I'd check my watch every so often to count the minutes until the bell rang for recess. But Baba Ji had a way of making me feel fully engaged and inspired throughout the whole event. The hours felt like minutes, and when it all ended, I wished it would carry on a little longer. This was because Baba Ji was really entertaining. His stories were exciting, and every piece of advice he gave had value. I realized that it was worth paying full attention to everything he said. And when things started getting complicated or a little too serious, he would slip in a perfectly timed joke that made everyone laugh, including him. As fancy and mighty and godlike as he was, it was not below the great guru to giggle at his own jokes.

At school the day following the *satsang*, my friend Miguel asked me what Baba Ji was like. I gave the exact answer that was expected.

"He was *so* funny and wise. He knows the answers for every question in the world!"

"That's so cool, man," replied an impressed Miguel.

But I knew in my heart that I had a more accurate answer to give Miguel. I was embarrassed to say it.

His actual superpower was . . . he made you feel special.

Chapter 2

A TOMATO IS A FRUIT

On my journey to where I am today, I've learned a lot about mastery. By definition, that is the goal of every thought leader who sets out on a quest to become a guru. You could say that Baba Ji was my first exposure to seeing the dormant potential that lies within every creator. Baba Ji was the template, the blueprint for me to realize my own capability of becoming a guru. But there's a big chasm between recognizing that you have potential as a creator and actually living it out IRL.

When you think of a spiritual guru, you may think of a psychic like the Three-Eyed Raven from *Game of Thrones*, or a wise old wizard like Gandalf from *The Lord of the Rings*. As a kid I wasn't able to bend spoons with my mind like that kid in *The Matrix*, either. I wanted a different superpower—something a little more down to Earth. I watched my parents commuting to work every day and decided that I wanted to start my own business to take control of my own destiny. The path to getting there was my own hero's journey.

Long before I knew what an influencer or thought leader was, I was just a typical big-dreaming high schooler fascinated with the internet.

I was certainly no miracle child genius with an Einstein-like IQ. You might have seen videos of those pimply Indian kids with thin-rimmed glasses that can calculate the square root of 137,464,729,474,674.97 in under 10 seconds without a calculator. It's a stereotype one learns to expect on an *India's Got Talent*–type TV show. Nope, I'm afraid I wasn't one of those dudes.

I did fairly well at school. Second-generation kids from immigrant families generally do. Because we'll be in some serious trouble at home if we don't work hard and "pull our socks up." I was always aware of the pressure of the responsibility I held. My grandparents sacrificed everything so that their future grandchildren could have the opportunities of the American dream. And my parents worked tirelessly and selflessly so that my little brother and I could have a fighting chance at making successes of ourselves.

From a young age, the path I was expected to take was made pretty clear. I had to work my butt off to get good grades so I could get into a respectable college, the kind that my parents could (very humbly) brag about. I'd have to choose between one of the universally accepted "respectable" careers—you know the ones . . . doctor, lawyer, accountant, etc. I tried my best to get excited about science and biology. But the truth was that there were three particular subjects that filled my mind with excitement. The first was relative automotive envisaging (RAV; more on this in a bit), the second was business, and the third was the internet.

For business and the internet, I had all the support in the world from my childhood friend Neil. He wasn't family per se, but our bond of friendship has lasted for decades. You've probably heard of him, Neil Patel—not only is he the author of the foreword for this book, but he's also one of the most famous digital marketing gurus on the planet! But before he was known as the marketing guru that he is today, he was just one of my friends in high school. And he was a pivotal force in my development of raw entrepreneurial ambition.

Today, Neil's a thought leader, industry pioneer, and *New York Times* bestselling author, and if you Google lists of the most influential people in digital marketing, you'll always find his name in the top five. He's helped companies like Amazon, NBC, General Motors, Hewlett-Packard, and Viacom grow their revenue. *The Wall Street Journal* named him a top influencer on the web, *Forbes* named him in their top 10 online marketer list, and *Entrepreneur Magazine* recognized him as having "created one of the 100 most brilliant companies in the world."[1] Just to go on a tiny bit more about my brilliant friend . . . he was recognized as a Top 100 entrepreneur under the age of 30 by President Obama and one of the Top 100 entrepreneurs under the age of 35 by the United Nations. He has even been awarded Congressional Recognition from the United States House of Representatives.

Neil and I competed a lot in high school (in a good way). We would challenge each other to do better than the other in our business class exams. We had a number of things in common, among them having a passion for business, being ambitious for our future, and sharing a love of computer stuff.

We became friends in 2002. These were the early days of the internet. And Neil was spending hundreds of hours trying to figure out this new-world online ecosystem. In many ways, he filled the missing big brother role in my life—pushing me to be the very best possible version of myself.

Just to give you a quick snapshot of what the online world looked like back in 2002:

1. MSN Search was the most popular search engine—second was Yahoo, and then Google (eek!).
2. Social media as we know it didn't exist. Mark Zuckerberg hadn't even thought of the idea of Facebook yet.
3. We used to log on to the internet with 56k modems that made the "eeee deee di-di-di-deee" sound. (Some great nostalgia for

those who were there. If you weren't around yet, delight your parents by asking them to do an impression!)

Back then, the internet was completely new terrain, and my friend Neil was one of those brave souls determined to work it all out and create a playbook for online hustling. He was my mentor and taught me all that he could. He had already started a side hustle selling products on this new website called eBay, which was quickly gaining popularity. Neil showed me how it all worked, and I decided to jump in too. We'd buy the items in bulk, then resell them for a profit. The more we experimented, the more success we had. But when my dad found out about my side hustle, he wasn't all that pleased. So he made me stop the venture immediately. Still, I made a couple hundred bucks off the experiment! This was enough to show me that there was definitely money to be made with this whole internet thing. But luckily, I didn't stop there. You see, I had a cousin who was a walking billboard for living the American dream. I called him "Ferrari Sanjay," and he was my biggest inspiration.

While business and the internet are fairly common, you may not be familiar with the subject of RAV. That's because I made up that fancy-sounding name so I wouldn't sound like such a predictably obvious teenager. In essence, at the core of the subject of RAV was my older cousin Sanjay's Ferrari. He was in his 20s and had a 2000 silver Ferrari 360 Spider. It was the coolest thing I'd ever seen.

With the mindset of a high school kid, I had decided I would definitely get one someday too. And in silver, too, because it looked awesome. I would do whatever it would take. I never considered it an impossible dream. I was going to do it. The thing is, Cousin Sanjay driving around in his silver Ferrari, living the life of the rich and famous, had never set foot inside a college classroom.

Indian kid not going to college? Scandalous!

No, seriously. Like a real-deal scandal!

But no one in the community was judging Ferrari Sanjay. And his parents were certainly not ashamed of him. Sanjay was the very image of success. He was the immigrant poster child for the American dream. This got the cogs turning in my high school teenager brain.

THE DRIVER OF FERRARIS

I wasn't sure what I wanted to be when I grew up. But I did know that I wanted to be just like Ferrari Sanjay. In many ways, like Neil, he felt like the big brother I was always desperately longing for in my family. At least, he fulfilled that archetype for me, since I never had a big brother of my own. I wanted whatever occupation would give me a silver Ferrari as part of the outcome, and I would do anything to get it.

At 17 years old, feeling finally old enough to get my own Ferrari, I spoke to Sanjay. It made sense to me that he was the right person in my life to seek advice from. I hadn't connected the idea or the word at this point, but to 17-year-old me, Cousin Sanjay, the Driver of Ferraris, was a *guru*.

Growing up as an American kid with an Indian heritage, the concept of following a spiritual guru was a big part of our family life. Gurus were elders that possessed incredible wisdom, and their devoted followers would seek advice from their guru for all of life's questions. Take Baba Ji, for instance. He didn't even need to advertise. Somehow, as if by magic, people gravitated toward his message organically.

Gurus were always in high demand because they were the only ones brave enough to answer the big questions like "What's the meaning of life?" or "What happens after death?" (Throughout this book, I'll sprinkle in some of the most important life and business lessons I learned from these traditional Indian gurus.)

Although the traditional Indian gurus were close to infinitely wise and seemed to have an immediate answer or story for any question under the sun, they were not really in the business of business. Gurus were in the business of life. They helped advise and guide us on how to live our lives with purpose, value, and positive direction.

But at this particular age, fresh out of school and ambitiously beginning my journey to seek a playbook for career success, I needed to find a guru of Ferraris. And that was Cousin Sanjay.

In truth, just like pretty much any human on this planet would, I hoped that Sanjay would share with me a secret get-rich-quick playbook. I hoped he would say something like, "My dear cousin AJ, don't tell anyone this secret. OK? All you have to do is x, then y, then do a little bit of z—and then sit back and watch the millions roll into your bank account." Remember celebrity cookbooks? I was salivating over Sanjay's playbook that would give me the recipes to cook up my own silver Ferrari!

However, his suggestion wasn't quite what I hoped for.

He told me I needed . . . a *job*. Of all things, Cousin Sanjay, why on earth would a daring entrepreneur like me want to settle for a nine-to-five?

Oh, how naive I was.

THE JOB THAT WAS MORE THAN A JOB

I took Sanjay's advice—he was my guru, after all—and he helped get me my first "real job." The position was as a telephone salesman for the Mike Ferry Organization, which came highly recommended by Sanjay. My job was to sell tickets to real estate agents for seminars where they would learn how to advance their careers. On the face of it, it seemed like a pretty standard telesales gig. The product happened to be event tickets, but that seemed fairly irrelevant to me at the time. It could have been magazine subscriptions, vacuum cleaners, or cans of beans. I was eager to sell anything to make money. But selling event tickets forced me to learn one of the most important skills on the path to becoming a guru.

Mike Ferry started out as a residential real estate agent in California. His is an industry that attracts many ambitious hopefuls. In California alone, there are over 200,000 active real estate agents.

Most of these 200,000 hopefuls would consider Mike as having reached the pinnacle of success in real estate. He had done something that very few real estate agents were doing—he had *positioned himself* in such a way that it was clear to everyone who interacted with him that he had already reached the top of the mountain. He was living the dream of millions of real estate agents around the globe, and *he knew it*. He exuded confidence, charisma, and leadership skills.

While the other industry leaders sat back and enjoyed the view from the top of the Mountain of Success, Mike recognized that there was another, even greater mountain for him to climb and conquer. He knew that his successes were stepping stones for a far more rewarding playbook—a far more powerful business model. Mike decided to launch his own company, the Mike Ferry Organization. To his colleagues' surprise, this was not an organization that sold real estate. It was a real estate coaching business. At the time, the Mike Ferry Organization was a $50 million company with tens of thousands of clients. And today, Mike Ferry is still recognized as one of the most influential people in the entire real estate profession. Even though I had no plans to become a real estate agent, I found Mike's story fascinating and inspiring.

A TOMATO IS A FRUIT

Before I earned my cubicle and telephone, I was put through rigorous sales training. Looking back, I think this was part of Cousin Sanjay's wisdom. Learning the skills of selling is perhaps the most important skill to master for just about any career there is. Whatever industry you are in, and whatever position you hold, you will need to at some point be a salesperson. While I thought I was just dialing for dollars, what I didn't realize is that I was actually learning an unexpected secret: Sales is all about having leverage.

Archimedes said it best: "Give me a lever long enough and a fulcrum on which to place it, and I will move the world." To get the type of sales leverage I'm talking about, you need to be consciously aware of your personal brand's positioning. You see, this is where Mike Ferry was a Yoda-level Jedi master. Positioning, in case you aren't familiar, is how you define and present your business. It's the process of occupying a distinctive place in the audience's mind relative to competitors. Good positioning shows people why you're different. This differentiation is reinforced through consistent messaging, visual identity, and customer experience. All these factors combine to create your brand's positioning in the mind of the customer.

Since most of you reading this have probably used Google and are at least a little familiar with the concept of SEO, you can think of positioning like the ranking system on Google. Everyone wants to be on the first page, because then they will get the most traffic. The difference between being on page one or page two is crucial! Ask yourself—when was the last time you scrolled down to the bottom of the page and clicked the little "Next" button? Positioning can be your secret weapon.

Mike Ferry knew this secret. He positioned himself as a high-demand authority. When he answered questions, he didn't defer to anyone else—he made definitive statements that held water, based on his successful track record and decades of experience. Mike didn't need to chase clients or try to attract them, like most real estate trainers. Instead, he let his positioning do all the heavy lifting for him. Essentially, good positioning flips the script: Instead of working harder for small gains, you use strategic branding, pricing, and networking to create big wins from smaller efforts. It's the twenty-first-century updated version of the old adage, "Work smarter, not harder." Mike Ferry showed me that positioning is all about showcasing your unique value so effectively that clients seek you out, pay more for your expertise, and unlock new opportunities you couldn't reach before. Working with Mike taught me that expertise alone isn't enough. There's an inner journey every successful authority must take. From uncertainty to confidence, from following to leading. Mike had walked the Guru's Journey himself, transforming from a real estate agent into an industry icon.

Over the days, weeks, and months of endless phone calls, my bank account was looking pretty healthy. But there was something I was getting that was far beyond the value of the sales commissions. I was gaining something priceless from working in proximity to Mike Ferry, a true business guru. I was beginning to realize that due to Mike's strong positioning, he wasn't simply selling his brand or reputation; his positioning in the marketplace was the secret sauce that made him one of the most attractive real estate trainers in the country. What he was selling was far more valuable than the measly 3% standard commission most agents earn on a home sale. He taught me that there was something gurus could sell that was of much higher value: *knowledge*.

Knowledge

Mike Ferry had a brain packed with a huge amount of knowledge on real estate and its many different aspects. The kind of knowledge that he had was of incredibly high value to anyone working in the industry. Using his techniques, I watched our clients go from struggling to thriving by following his advice. His audience—which encompassed just about every real estate agent in the industry—was eager for this knowledge and perceived it as an investment in their future.

His audience wasn't looking for get-rich-quick real estate schemes. Instead, they were ready to finally learn the ins and outs of real estate for themselves. Thanks to Mike's brilliant positioning strategy, he was touted as the predominant thought leader, and his knowledge was highly coveted by other agents.

Experience

Mike Ferry was a teacher, but not the typical kind of teacher. Mike had spent literally decades of his life to gain the experience he had. Many can go broke several times in their lives while on the journey to gain career experience. But Mike Ferry was able to offer a "golden ticket." In his seminars, he would share his most important experiences and the lessons he learned from them. The value of this to his audience was that in just a few hours, days, or weeks (depending on the program), they could potentially save years trying to reinvent the wheel. Instead, Mike just handed them a blueprint to unlock bigger opportunities in the world of real estate.

Wisdom

Society values wisdom as one of the most precious assets an individual can have. True wisdom is not a common trait. It takes a special mind to combine knowledge with experience and provide the alchemy to turn it into wisdom. One dictionary says wisdom is "about knowing when and how to use your knowledge, being able to put situations in perspective, and how to impart it to others."[2] Mike Ferry was indeed a wise man, and he understood that this gift was a valuable commodity to a large audience.

One of the most frequently quoted teachers of wisdom in history is the Chinese philosopher Confucius. On the topic of wisdom, Confucius said, "By three methods we may learn wisdom: first, by reflection, which is noblest; second, by imitation, which is easiest; and third, by experience, which is the bitterest."

Mike Ferry was able to offer the second kind—the opportunity for imitation—and as Confucius correctly pointed out, this is the easiest route to gaining wisdom. In every sphere of our lives, perhaps nothing is more highly valued than the opportunity of something being "easy." It's what we all seek, and something we rarely find. Although you've probably understood my explanation about wisdom, I can't resist adding in one more of my favorite definitions for wisdom that I've seen. It's rather brilliant in its silliness. *Knowledge* is knowing a tomato is a fruit. *Wisdom* is knowing not to put it in a fruit salad.

As I continued to gain experience within the company—from my sales call conversations with potential clients, to attending talks and seminars, to gathering insights from my colleagues—I began to see an even deeper picture. I began to understand the psychology of Mike Ferry's positioning and why his business model was so incredibly attractive. I began to realize why my job as a salesman was surprisingly easy. Whether I was selling the $300 public talk tickets or the $1,000-plus-per-month seminars and courses, or anything in between, I found that there was little need for "hard selling." I wasn't sweating and scrambling to convince potential clients with every sales trick in the book. What I found was that the vast majority of people I spoke to were very much aware of Mike Ferry and his wonderful reputation. Mike had literally hundreds of thousands of followers (this was before the age of social media, so I use this term in its original sense). These followers were deeply loyal to him. It made me think of religious followers, even cult followers (without the negative connotation that often comes with the word "cult").

People that followed Mike Ferry adored him. They trusted him. They saw him the way I saw him: Mike Ferry was not just another real estate guy. Mike Ferry was a *guru*.

Chapter 3

SPIRITUAL GURUS VS. BUSINESS GURUS

He who controls others may be powerful, but he who
has mastered himself is mightier still.

—Lao Tzu

Before I get too deep into telling you my backstory, I want to interrupt the monologue so I can catch you up to speed on how I came to understand the secrets of how gurus gain adoration and influence in our modern world. The term "guru" started out as a powerful signifier of respect for leaders of Eastern religions like our family's guru, Baba Ji. In our modern context, we've westernized the term, so to speak, by expanding its usage to refer to anyone who commands respect for their mastery of or expertise in a subject. Because traditional gurus were seen as wise and authoritative, the word naturally extended to anyone who had deep knowledge in a particular area.

Here's what I realized growing up around spiritual gurus. They had something most business experts are missing. People actually wanted to hear from them. So I started asking myself a question. What if business gurus could create that same kind of magnetic pull? (That includes you, dear reader.)

People follow spiritual gurus because they believe these guys have a direct line to something bigger, like God, universal truth, or whatever you want to call it. They don't have to prove themselves the same way businesspeople do.

Business gurus, on the other hand, have to earn their authority. They rely on content, social proof, and strategic positioning to build trust. While spiritual gurus are often granted status by those seeking guidance, business gurus must prove themselves over time through testimonials, case studies, and demonstrated expertise.

Both types of gurus become successful based on their followers' belief in their authority, but spiritual gurus rise to prominence from their followers' faith and perception. Business gurus attempt to create a similar effect—leveraging credibility, symbols of success, and strategic storytelling to make people believe in their expertise in the same way spiritual followers believe in their guru's wisdom.

Here's what hit me. I grew up believing Baba Ji had this almost godlike authority. As a kid, I was genuinely scared he could read my mind. My parents had conditioned me from a young age to revere him, and that sense of awe shaped the way I saw power and influence. While it frightened me then, looking back, I can see how deeply it shaped my thinking about how powerful leaders influence their audiences—not just through what they say, but through how they are perceived.

The real secret behind understanding how gurus influence their followers lies in how they position themselves. When clients want to grow their online sphere of influence and find an audience for their work, they ask me to help them refine their digital marketing strategies. When this happens, one of the most powerful lessons that I teach them is the difference between organic and strategic positioning. Organic positioning is authority that develops naturally through community recognition, word of mouth, and demonstrated mastery, without deliberate marketing strategies. Strategic positioning just means you're being smart about how you show up online. You're not leaving it to chance. You're deliberately building how people see you.

This is something that I learned by comparing the spiritual concept of being a guru to the revamped twenty-first-century context, which by definition has been expanded to include business mentors like Mike Ferry and Neil Patel. When I realized how I could use my spiritual upbringing to help my clients gain traction and momentum in their businesses, it felt like capturing lightning in a bottle! The power of these connections has helped me teach my clients how to transform their brands and grow their businesses to new heights.

Despite both having gurus, there's a big difference between the spiritual world and the business world. Mike Ferry doesn't adopt a full lotus position onstage like Baba Ji, and Baba Ji would probably be a terrible sales trainer when compared to a true sales wizard like Mike Ferry. But aside from the obvious differences, the real magic that makes gurus so magnetic to their followers is how they present themselves to their audience. Spiritual gurus like Baba Ji rely on organic positioning. Meaning, they appeal to the emotional needs of their followers. He doesn't do anything to seek attention or market himself; he relies solely on the strength of his wisdom to authentically promote his brand through the "network effect." His word-of-mouth fanbase is driven by purpose rather than profit.

Mike Ferry (and business gurus as a whole), on the other hand, positions himself using strategic content and social proof. By interacting with his followers in the online digital sphere through engaging and thoughtful content, personalized phone calls, social media posts, and a strong digital presence on his website, he appeals to the unique pain points of his audience. Business gurus succeed by building credibility through testimonials and proven case studies that demonstrate their cutting-edge expertise. By promoting these successes on social media, they scale their influence to the masses and use it to generate more leads on a consistent basis over time.

For instance, Mike Ferry built his brand over the past few decades using traditional marketing. Good old-fashioned cold calls, in-person visits to real estate offices, and live training sessions. His success was driven by direct engagement and face-to-face credibility long before social media became the norm. But like everyone else, he has adapted to learning how to leverage social media and digital platforms to expand his influence. While his foundation remains rooted in traditional methods, he integrates modern strategies—sharing testimonials, case studies, and strategic content—to continue scaling his reach and generating leads in today's digital landscape. He did it strategically using modern mediums to get people to discover him and his message.

You may now be wondering, *AJ, is there a way to do both kinds of positioning?*

The best business leaders should balance organic authenticity with strategic positioning, ensuring their message resonates deeply with their audience. In essence, they can capture the same type of market share through their genuine charisma and wisdom while simultaneously leveraging modern marketing tools. By adopting a tandem approach, business leaders can develop a philosophy-driven message that combines practical solutions with a deeper purpose.

Spiritual gurus become highly sought after because their followers resonate with their focus on sharing passionate, heartfelt messages of inner transformation that lead them on a pathway to self-realization. These teachings often transcend the current paradigms of their day. Similarly, business gurus can also advance rapidly in their industry by playing the role of the contrarian, based on the conviction of their strong beliefs and new ways of thinking about old problems. There's a reason why the entrepreneurs on ABC's *Shark Tank* are highly lauded for bucking conventional business norms and taking risks on emergent products and big-dreaming, first-time entrepreneurs. The best, most successful business gurus often take huge risks because they know the payoff can be great. To be considered a guru, you have to do things (such as taking calculated risks) that defy conventional wisdom.

THE POWER OF COMMUNITY

The cornerstone of any guru's playbook is fostering a spirit of belonging and a sense of organic community within their audience. But how these two different types of gurus achieve that varies. For spiritual gurus, the shared collective experience of helping their followers feel something new wakes them up. Having transcendent spiritual experiences within the safety of a tight-knit community allows them the safety and freedom to create beautiful moments that uplift their community members and take them out of the monotony of their everyday lives.

Business gurus seek to do the same, but the tools they use to get there are different. For instance, a shared private Facebook community may help followers find a shared common bond as they all work together to solve similar pain points. Successful business gurus create a "platform culture" that helps their followers find other like-minded people who can grow through online platforms and membership communities that mirror the ecstatic experience of attending a spiritual retreat. The takeaway for anyone seeking to replicate the success of gurus like Mike Ferry is to focus on cultivating authentic relationships with their audience that prioritize depth over surface-level sales conversations. A true business guru knows that the most important ingredient of their success is building deeply rooted communities.

Most spiritual gurus operate through philanthropy and volunteers, which become the backbone of their communities. Business gurus prioritize this slightly differently, by leveraging profit from courses, consulting, and live events. Once a guru generates enough revenue, they can then reinvest their time, energy, and expertise into mentorship, community enrichment activities, and service work. While the path to getting there may look very different, the end result is often very similar: service to their community. Both spiritual and business gurus desire to leave a lasting legacy of impact and service that outlives them. The real difference isn't in their methods; it's in how they navigate the Guru's Journey. Spiritual gurus often have their transformation validated by ancient traditions. Business gurus must prove their evolution through results, testimonials, and market success. Both paths require the same internal shifts: from doubt to certainty, from student to teacher. Often, this is done by creating pedagogy or branding elements that are highly personalized and very difficult to copy. While a spiritual guru may leave behind scriptures or texts that establish their deepest, innermost philosophy, a business guru will focus on building a company that lives on after their death through strategic branding elements that cement their digital legacy. They may wish to create evergreen digital assets that teach and inspire their community, even after they die.

So how can content creators looking to build an empire start applying spiritual principles to their business?

I teach my clients that authenticity is the key to success. Embodying values that align with your followers' beliefs is the fastest way to create long-lasting relationships that foster organic community growth. When you find people who are willing to come together to uphold a similar philosophy, it is really powerful. The strength of community amplifies your message, and using the power of social media to do the heavy lifting for you can exponentially increase the size of your community. Just make sure that you focus on creating depth by prioritizing serving your audience over monetization.

In this East-meets-West mashup, it is important to remember that one strategy isn't necessarily better than the other. Business leaders looking to build a personal brand around their expertise should combine the spiritual and business strategies I shared earlier to maximize their impact. A successful personal brand blends both approaches—leveraging digital strategies while maintaining authenticity, values, and community impact for sustainable influence.

The foundation of thought leadership is built on authenticity and fostering deep relationships with your community. Remember, true authority isn't manufactured or built overnight. Real transformation, just like becoming a guru, is a process that takes years to master and perfect.

Chapter 4
FROM HOMES TO HOME PAGES

You can't connect the dots looking forward; you can only connect them looking backward.

—Steve Jobs[3]

OK, now back to your regularly scheduled programming . . .

Success has a funny way of sneaking up on you. One day, you're the new kid fumbling through sales calls, and the next thing you know, you're sitting at the top of the leaderboard at the Mike Ferry Organization. The same nervous energy that made me overthink every word during my first week had somehow transformed into the confidence that was now consistently bringing in thousands of dollars in commissions every two weeks. I was good at this—really good. But something inside me knew this wasn't my final destination.

That's when Ferrari Sanjay hit me with this crazy opportunity. "AJ," he said during one of our regular catch-ups, "I've been thinking." When

Sanjay starts a sentence that way, you know something huge is coming. "What if we took what Mike Ferry is doing for real estate and expanded it to all kinds of business professionals?"

The way Sanjay laid out his vision was mesmerizing. He had this natural ability to make you see possibilities you never even considered before. His words painted pictures of packed seminar rooms and transformed lives. I could see it so clearly. He could become the Indian Tony Robbins. When Sanjay spoke, you didn't just hear the words; you felt the energy of what could be.

After two years at the Mike Ferry Organization, I packed up my life and pointed my car toward Las Vegas, where we would establish our headquarters. At 20 years old, being in Vegas felt both exciting and slightly illegal. I found a small studio apartment right behind the Wynn. Now, that might sound fancy, but let me paint you a more accurate picture—my daily commute involved carefully stepping over crack pipes on the sidewalk. Welcome to the real Vegas, kid. Our office, though, was a different story. Located on Howard Hughes Parkway, it had that professional shine that made you feel like you were part of something bigger. I'd get there early every morning, usually before the sun was up, ready to make calls across different time zones. Our client list read like a Vegas fever dream—real estate agents, loan officers, CEOs, world-class poker players, and even stage hypnotists. Each day brought new challenges and new possibilities.

Then came what I like to call our "digital awakening." One of Sanjay's coaching clients introduced us to his son, a tech-savvy guy. As we walked into his apartment, there he was, perched in front of his computer, talking about something called Web 2.0. "Social media," he said. "Twitter. Start a blog." He spoke about these things like they were the keys to a kingdom we didn't even know existed. It felt like he was casting magic spells, using some secret language, the etymology of which I didn't know. It was a new kind of internet where everyone could share their thoughts, others could comment and share, and ideas could grow and reach people around the world.

I didn't fully grasp what Web 2.0 meant at first, but I could sense its potential. Being the most computer-savvy person in our office (which wasn't saying much), I volunteered to take on this mysterious digital project. Most days found me hunched over my computer, teaching myself the basics of everything from website building to simple coding. It was like learning a new language—one made of HTML tags and CSS stylesheets. Just as I was starting to get my digital sea legs under me, the real world came crashing in.

When the 2008 economic crisis hit, it hit hard. Our company, like so many others, couldn't weather the storm. Suddenly, I found myself with empty pockets and an even emptier sense of direction. We got rid of the Vegas office space. I moved back into my parents' house and commuted to Sanjay's place to keep working in his pool house. I was starting to feel like a failure. But sometimes, rock bottom comes with a silver lining. A friend handed me a book that would change everything: *The 4-Hour Workweek* by Tim Ferriss. Between those pages, I discovered a world of digital opportunity I never knew existed—one that would make my amateur attempts at marketing look like preparation for something much bigger.

My relationship with Sanjay was already showing cracks when fate decided to throw one more curveball. A car accident with my brother, Jason, left me with a broken foot. Nothing too serious, but try navigating driving 45 minutes back and forth to your office with a cast. Driving became harder and harder, so I was forced to stay put and just work from home. Little did I know that my next chapter was just beginning.

TWO NEILS ARE BETTER THAN ONE

Life has a funny way of bringing people back into your orbit when you need them most. During this time, I reconnected with my long-lost high school friend Neil Patel. What started as a casual catchup turned into hours of conversation that would reshape my entire career path.

Back in high school, Neil had always stood out. While the rest of us were busy trying to navigate the awkward chaos of teenage life, Neil was already 10 steps ahead. His mind was wired to see patterns and opportunities where others saw only confusion. Even then, it was clear he was destined for something big. So, it came as no surprise that Neil found his calling in digital marketing. While most of us were using the internet to chat with friends or download music, Neil saw it as a business frontier waiting to be explored. By the time we reconnected, he had become what Mike Ferry was to real estate—a true guru in his field. Neil was the SEO mastermind, the visionary every aspiring digital marketer followed with almost religious devotion. He had positioned himself in much the same way that Mike had, and the results of his success spoke for themselves.

We became friends and started teaching each other what we knew. Over countless lunches at Romano's Macaroni Grill and late-night conversations at coffee shops, Neil opened my eyes to the world of digital marketing. He taught me the technical foundations like how to set up a blog, optimize content, and navigate the complex world of SEO. In return, I shared what I knew best: the psychology of success and the power of mindset. At first, Neil was skeptical about these "soft skills," but he soon realized how dramatically they could impact both his business approach and bottom line.

So I started my first blog, Persuasive.net, where I could test out all this stuff I was learning. I combined my sales experience with newly acquired technical skills to create content that bridged the gap between traditional persuasion and digital marketing. What started as a passion project quickly turned into a showcase of hybrid knowledge—copywriting, email marketing, SEO, content strategy, web development, user experience, and data analysis. What surprised me most was how quickly it grew. A blog,

I discovered, is essentially a public journal that can reach anyone, anywhere. When you create valuable content and optimize it properly, amazing things can happen. One day, I nearly fell out of my chair when I saw that Tony Robbins had tweeted one of my articles to his followers. Soon after, the blog was pulling in nearly 30,000 visitors a month.

Then came a revelation that changed everything: you could package knowledge into a digital product. But more importantly, I realized something fascinating about selling stuff online. Sales pages are essentially virtual salespeople. Instead of me making outbound calls one person at a time like I did at the Mike Ferry Organization, I could create a single sales page that would work 24/7, delivering the same persuasive presentation to thousands of visitors. It was the complete opposite of my cold-calling days. The principles were the same—understanding psychology, building trust, handling objections—but now I was doing it at scale, with visitors coming inbound to me.

I put this insight to work immediately. I took my expertise in persuasive communication and created a seven-day program, initially as a print book, then as an ebook. Selling it for $19.95, I generated around $800 seemingly out of thin air. It was mind-blowing. I was literally monetizing my thoughts, and my strategically written sales page was doing all the heavy lifting, thanks to the magic leverage of positioning.

Through these online experiments, I was learning valuable lessons about technical positioning. SEO rankings, high traffic, well-designed websites, and a strong cohesive online narrative all help to position brands as more authoritative. These skills were useful beyond just selling $20 ebooks; they were the key that unlocked doors that had major earning potential.

The words "get a real job" seemed at this point to follow me around like a persistent echo. First it was Sanjay, telling teenage me to forget about Ferraris and focus on steady work. Now here was Neil, suggesting I needed a nine-to-five while my digital dreams took shape. The difference? This time, I wasn't rolling my eyes. My blog was growing, and watching those first few ebook sales come in felt like magic. But my bank account had a different story to tell. Those sporadic PayPal notifications weren't exactly keeping pace with rent and groceries. Reality has a way of cutting through your entrepreneurial daydreams with a sharp knife called bills.

As I sat there digesting Neil's advice, something clicked. I already had years of real estate experience under my belt. I understood the industry, spoke its language, and knew its pain points. Why not merge that knowledge with my newfound digital marketing skills?

It wasn't about giving up on the dream—it was about being smart enough to build a bridge between my past and my future. This train of thought led me to another Neil I knew: Neil Schwartz, whom I remembered from my Mike Ferry days. Neil Schwartz, a top broker and owner of one of the leading Century 21 Real Estate franchises in the country, was also one of Mike's head coaches. If Mike Ferry was his guru, maybe there was something I could learn from him too.

THE GURU'S GURU

With all the knowledge I gained from my old school buddy Neil, I started seeing the online world in a completely new light. The internet had evolved from its cute early days of chat rooms and basic websites into something revolutionary. This wasn't just a new technology anymore—it was a gold rush. Silicon Valley entrepreneurs were becoming billionaires overnight, and investors were throwing unbelievable amounts of money at anything that might be the "next big thing."

The game had changed entirely. Smartphones meant that nearly everyone on the planet was walking around with a computer in their pocket (a far cry from the days when the most exciting thing on your phone was a game called Snake). But perhaps the biggest revolution of all was search engines and social media. It created an entirely new eco-system where fortunes could be made and lost, where new industries appeared almost daily, and where marketing would never be the same.

I felt like I had accidentally prepared for this moment. Between my high school experiments with the early digital world and the invaluable insights from Neil Patel, I had knowledge that many others were still struggling to grasp. The question was: How could I merge this digital expertise with my real estate career?

This brought me back to Neil Schwartz. He wasn't just another real estate agent—he was at the very top of his game and earning serious money. Under Mike Ferry's guidance, Neil had built a multitiered busi-ness empire. Instead of grinding it out as a solo agent, he had an entire team of successful agents working for him. Mike Ferry had taught him how to scale like an entrepreneur, and in the process, Neil Schwartz had learned how to position himself as a guru. He was now passing Mike's teachings on to others, creating his own following of devoted agents.

That's when it hit me: If Neil Schwartz was a guru, then what was Mike Ferry? He was something more than just a guru: He was a *guru's guru*. Looking at Mike Ferry's organization like a pyramid (not the scam kind), Mike sat at the top. One level below him were influential figures like Neil Schwartz, who were authorities in their own right with their own loyal followers. Mike Ferry wasn't just teaching agents; he was cre-ating other teachers, which was helping his life-changing knowledge get shared exponentially with the real estate industry.

Seeing the opportunity, Neil Schwartz took me under his wing, agreeing to mentor me in real estate while I helped modernize his digital marketing approach. Under his guidance, I developed and executed his marketing strategy. The results were impressive. I helped grow his pres-ence across multiple channels—from social media to blog posts to email campaigns—working tirelessly to generate top-quality content that posi-tioned Neil as an industry thought leader.

My instincts about digital marketing proved right. Neil Schwartz's early investment in his online presence laid the foundation for massive growth. Today, his website proudly proclaims: "My agents have closed over 340 transactions in the last 45 days and generated $4.5 million in commissions." Numbers don't lie—the digital transformation worked.

While helping Neil Schwartz leverage digital marketing and position himself as a thought leader in his field to dominate his local real estate market, I was discovering my own path forward. The same tools I used to build his online presence were opening doors I never knew existed. My world was about to expand far beyond real estate, and the lessons I learned from the guru's guru were about to be put to use in ways I never expected . . .

FROM A SEED TO A SINGLE GRAIN

Success in the digital world has a way of snowballing. As my work with Neil Schwartz grew, so did my reputation. Neil Patel started seeing more potential in me and took me under his wing. Soon, I was outgrowing my role at Neil Schwartz's company. The online world was calling, and I answered by diving into digital marketing. Neil began introducing me to his clients who needed help with something I'd come to realize was the purest form of positioning: SEO. My work with Mike Ferry had taught me that his guru positioning was literally the same thing as how Google strategically positioned websites based on rankings. The higher your positioning, the more traffic you received. This was a momentous awakening for me that helped me see that SEO is literally the art and science of positioning websites in the digital landscape.

While Mike Ferry had taught me about positioning yourself as an authority in the real estate world, SEO was about positioning in its most concrete form—actually determining where your website appears in search results. I used to joke that I had become a "reverse engineer" instead of the traditional engineer my parents had hoped for. You see, while traditional engineers start with a problem and build something new to solve it, I was working backward—looking at Google's search results, figuring out why certain websites were positioned at the top, and then re-creating those success patterns for my clients.

The work involved helping websites achieve better positioning on search engines like Google by optimizing their content and building quality backlinks—essentially, votes of confidence from other websites. Just like how Mike Ferry had built his authority through endorsements from industry leaders, websites built their authority through endorsements (links) from other respected sites.

For instance, one of Neil Patel's clients was in the credit card processing field. We'd strategically position phrases like "top 10 merchant services" or "best credit card processing" on other websites, linking back to our client's site. Think of it like a popularity contest, where each link is a vote, and the quality of the vote depends on how you position the endorsement. Since about 70% of users click on the top three search results, getting those top positions wasn't just about visibility—it was about dominating the digital landscape. Each ranking improvement was a direct reflection of how well we'd positioned the site in Google's eyes and, ultimately, in the eyes of potential customers.

This success in digital positioning, along with the skills I had developed from working for Neil, led me to launch my own internet business, which I proudly named Cash Cow Media LLC. While keeping Neil as a client, I started building my own websites. I was working smarter, not harder. Instead of trying to position myself one phone call at a time, I created review websites that Google would automatically position in front of people actively searching for solutions.

I started with what I knew best: real estate services. On my blog AgentDeals.net, I wrote detailed reviews of tools that real estate agents needed, like Mojo Dialer (a system for making sales calls) and RedX

Expired Leads (a service that finds houses that didn't sell). With my content properly positioned for Google, readers would find my reviews naturally when searching for these tools. When they decided to buy through my special tracking links, I earned a commission—without ever having to make a pitch. Instead of chasing customers one by one, my properly positioned content was drawing them to me.

The portfolio grew as I spotted new opportunities in emerging markets. I launched AllElectronicCigaretteReviews.com when e-cigarettes were just becoming popular, targeting people searching for terms like "best electronic cigarettes," "e-cigarette reviews," and "how to quit smoking." I also created TheTruthAboutOnlineDating.com (partially inspired by my own adventures in digital romance), which targeted searches like "best dating sites," "online dating advice," and "top dating sites reviews."

Despite knowing little about these niches initially, I followed the same formula: Create honest, detailed reviews, optimize for the right keywords, and help people make informed decisions. My top-secret guru positioning strategy worked beautifully! Each site was soon generating $3,000-$4,000 in monthly commissions. Basically, I was getting paid to be a trusted digital advisor in these spaces. Neil saw me gaining momentum in my business and introduced me to several of his venture capitalist friends. Here I was, building this portfolio of "digital real estate"—websites that were generating passive income just like rental properties, but without the headaches of tenants or maintenance. These venture capitalists were interested in investing in my growing empire, but Neil had a different suggestion.

He then introduced me to his cousin, Sujan Patel, who was cut from the same entrepreneurial cloth as us. We instantly clicked and worked really well together. I focused on sales and business development while Sujan brought his expertise in SEO strategy, technical execution, and natural leadership skills. He was an incredibly sharp business owner and marketer. Together, we merged our business into an entity called Single Grain Digital Marketing in 2011. The business took off like a rocket. Soon, we had a slew of clients ranging from Fortune 500 companies like Salesforce, Intuit, and Sony to small businesses like Bidet King and 24HourCaskets. (Everyone poops and dies, right?)

Our reputation grew as we helped companies climb to those coveted top three spots on Google. Whether clients wanted to rank for competitive terms like "cloud computing," "T-shirts," or "insurance quotes," we developed strategies that worked. We created detailed case studies of our successes, which only accelerated our growth.

The business evolved beyond just driving traffic—we started analyzing how users interacted with websites. We tracked what they clicked on, how far they scrolled, and other behaviors. Using that data, we adjusted website layouts, changed colors, and optimized elements to encourage more clicks and guide users to the checkout page. These changes increased conversion rates and, ultimately, boosted revenue for our clients. Our success caught the attention of major publications, and I found myself writing expert opinions on *Forbes*, *Entrepreneur Magazine*, *Social Media Examiner*, and many others. When Andrew Warner, founder of Mixergy, invited me to share my story on his platform—a place that had featured entrepreneurs like Gary Vaynerchuk and Jimmy Wales of Wikipedia—I was surprised and a little out of my depth. In my mind, I wasn't anywhere near their level. But my invite onto the show confirmed to me that my positioning had been on par with his other guests—in other words, my crazy entrepreneurial plan was working.

This journey taught me the profound importance of having a strong web presence. Your website isn't just a digital business card; it's your home base, your conversion engine, and your brand's heartbeat. It's where you own the experience, collect valuable data, and build lasting relationships with your audience. While social media platforms come and go, your website remains your digital foundation where you can position yourself and your personal brand to stand out from the crowd. In a sea of talented competitors, your online positioning is the most important leverage in creating your limitless future.

Chapter 5

PERCEPTION OVER TALENT

The question is not what you look at, but what you see.
—Henry David Thoreau[4]

On a typical Friday morning in 2007, thousands of commuters made their subway commute to work, just as they did every other day of the week. Nothing appeared unusual about the scene. There was a busker standing just inside the L'Enfant Plaza Metro entrance. He wore a baseball cap and played the violin. At his feet was a small box with some coins nestled inside. Any donations from generous passersby would be greatly appreciated.

On this particular Friday morning, the violin-playing busker tried his best to entertain the crowds with his repertoire of the classics. He played his heart out for almost an hour, making his way through six classical pieces—from Bach to Massenet to Schubert. Over 1,000 people passed him by. Only seven people took the time to pause for a moment and appreciate a minute or two of his lovely playing. Once the rush hour crowds had subsided, the violinist counted the coins and notes in his box, and it added up to $52.17. It would have been just $32.17 if it weren't for one older gentleman who generously gave a $20 bill.

That same evening, there was another classical violin performance in Washington, but instead of underground, this was in an upscale performance venue. Joshua Bell was in town to perform at an almost instantly sold-out show. Bell was one of the finest talents in the classical music world, a true star. He'd achieved worldwide fame as a child prodigy and spent his life between performing in front of adoring crowds and fulfilling the iconic role of music director for Academy of St Martin in the Fields. Before he went onstage, there was hurried excitement from the audience. As his figure appeared from behind the curtain, and the crowds caught a glimpse of his legendary godlike hair, there was an eruption of enthusiastic applause. He flashed a warm but reserved smile to the crowd and pulled out his magnificent violin: a Stradivarius from 1713. The chance to see and hear such a rarefied multimillion-dollar instrument (yes, his violin costs millions of dollars) being played was worth the hefty ticket price alone. Many forked out far more than the already high admission price, buying overpriced aftermarket tickets from scalpers. The local theater scalpers knew there would be people willing to pay almost anything for the once-in-a-lifetime experience. After all, this was Joshua Bell!

The maestro took his final bow after the third standing ovation and encore. The audience chatted among themselves about how emotional it was to witness this level of talent. It was almost a spiritual experience for them. In the theater's foyer, all the kiosks were completely sold out of every Joshua Bell product on offer, from the expensive event programs to the piles of CDs.

Think about these two performances for a second: the busker and the maestro. What lessons can we take away from comparing these two musicians and their polar-opposite levels of career? Why does one musician hold so much esteem and influence over his audience, while the other plays in the cold, largely ignored, for enough cash to buy a warm lunch? What separates the two?

Pause for a minute to think about it.

Probably the most obvious answer is *talent*. The busker, like 99% of musicians, is good, but he's not skilled beyond the millions of other talented violinists out there. If he wanted to get to the lofty status of the great Joshua Bell, he would have needed to be born with an unusual talent in his DNA, and secondly, he would have needed to put in the exceptional amount of painstaking hours to practice and practice and practice. On the face of it, the maestro likely earned his fame by simply working harder than his peers and therefore becoming the best of the best of the best.

In fact, in a crazy world, if you put Joshua Bell in the place of that busker on that Friday afternoon, if you gave him a fake beard and no one knew who he was, there's no doubt about it—he would still draw a crowd of thousands, and the station would be filled with applause, hollering, and whistles.

There's a twist to the story. One that should lift your spirits, because despite the Bradley Cooper and Lady Gaga remake of *A Star Is Born*, stars are not fated by astrological birth charts; they are made through dedication and hard work.

This hypothetical story was actually a real-life social experiment. The busker and the maestro were both Joshua Bell.

Perception. The way others view, understand, and interpret you and your brand. Perception is the outcome of effective positioning, amplified by context and presentation.

The Washington Post had arranged this experiment to explore a fascinating question: In an ordinary setting at an ordinary hour, would people recognize extraordinary talent?[5] The answer was a resounding no.

But this isn't a story about how people can't appreciate good music. It's about something far more important—something that would change my entire understanding of how to build a successful business and brand.

This experiment reveals a crucial truth about the Guru's Journey: Your internal transformation means nothing without the right external context. You can have all the wisdom in the world, but if you don't position yourself properly, you'll remain invisible. The journey isn't just about becoming wise; it's about learning to package and present that wisdom.

It's about the power of perception.

Think about it. The same notes, played by the same virtuoso, on the same priceless instrument, could be worth either pocket change or hundreds of dollars per ticket.

Does context change how people see things?

For our purposes, context is the environment, framing, or situation that influences how your expertise is perceived and valued. Context dramatically impacts perception. This is something I like to refer to as the "Joshua Bell effect": the idea that context can completely transform the perceived value of something, regardless of its actual quality. It's the same guy, playing the same violin, with the same level of skill. But the outcome? Completely different. That's the power of context.

The amazing thing for aspiring gurus is that this idea extends far beyond classical music. Whether you're a violinist, a business guru, or anyone trying to make their mark in the world, the way people perceive you can matter just as much as—if not more than—your actual talent.

This story is perfect for anyone building their brand because nothing about Joshua Bell actually changed. Mr. Bell was the same virtuoso violinist, with the same million-dollar violin, giving the same masterful performance—but the perception completely changed based on the context of how his message was positioned. In the subway station, he's positioned himself as an ordinary busker, not worthy of so much as a second glance. Whereas in the state-of-the-art acoustic, ornately decorated concert hall, his brand is positioned as a genius-level musician, touted as a true virtuoso performer worth hundreds of dollars per ticket. People dress up to look their best to welcome him to their city's finest theater to perform. That's a big difference!

But this story reveals a deeper truth about positioning and perception. An expert isn't more knowledgeable just because they have a bigger platform, but they may be perceived as more influential if they have a larger audience. When I authored blog-post content for big sites like *Forbes* or Mixergy—the equivalent of the "digital concert hall"—they were more influential than my posts on Persuasive .net, even though they were the same material, coming from the same writer (me). The better-positioned website gave the perception that it was more valuable.

THE PERCEPTION PRINCIPLE

I see this "Joshua Bell effect" happen all the time in digital marketing. Just like Bell in the subway, there are incredibly talented experts who struggle to get noticed because they haven't created the right context for their expertise. And just like Bell in the concert hall, there are others who command premium prices and devoted followings because they understand how to frame their value.

This reminds me of Baba Ji's photo hanging in our living room. When his image hung on our wall, he was just a picture in a frame. But the moment he walked into a crowded auditorium for the *satsang*, the entire atmosphere changed. People fell silent. They hung on his every word. Same person, different context, completely different impact.

I was about to learn this lesson firsthand through my work with one of my earliest clients, Kimberly Snyder.

What happened next would teach me everything about how perception shapes success in the digital age. But before I tell you about

Kimberly's transformation, let me explain what I mean by perception in the modern world.

You see, in today's digital landscape, perception isn't just about how you look or what you say. It's about creating an entire brand ecosystem that positions you as the authority you truly are. Think of it like building your own concert hall—a place where your expertise can be properly showcased and appreciated. But instead of physical architecture, we're talking about digital architecture: your website, your social media presence, your content strategy, and most importantly, the way all these pieces work together to create a powerful perception of your brand.

FROM CELEBRITY SECRET TO GLOBAL BRAND

When I first met Kimberly Snyder, she had already achieved what many would consider the dream: She was the go-to nutritionist for Hollywood's elite, spending her days in their luxury kitchens, creating meal plans that kept them camera-ready. She was making $500 an hour and had even published a book called *The Beauty Detox Solution*. By all conventional measures, she was successful.

But there was a problem. Like a virtuoso confined to playing in a single room, Kimberly's impact was limited by the physical constraints of time and space. She could only be in one celebrity kitchen at a time. She had extraordinary knowledge that could help millions, but she was stuck in a one-to-one business model. Her book was selling but not at the level it could. She had the talent, but like Joshua Bell in the subway, she wasn't being perceived at her full value.

This is where the magic of digital transformation comes in through the power of positioning. Just as a concert hall provides the perfect acoustic and visual environment for a violin performance, the digital world offers tools to amplify your expertise and present it in its best light. But here's the key—you can't just throw up a website and expect people to recognize your brilliance. You need to orchestrate every element of your digital presence to position yourself to get the perception you want.

We started by creating a "digital concert hall" for Kimberly—not just a website, but a carefully designed personality-driven media brand, where every part of the experience worked together to showcase her value. The website was the main venue—the place everything pointed back to. But the real emotional connection happened through her email list. That became our backstage pass. We treated it like an indoctrination sequence—using storytelling, cliffhangers, and moments of vulnerability to reveal Kimberly's personality, build credibility, and create emotional investment. The blog offered regular performances: wellness tips, beauty insights, and seasonal recipes that kept people coming back. Social media sparked curiosity and widened the audience. We weren't just broadcasting information. We were carefully shaping perception in order to position Kimberly as the relatable, trusted guide in wellness, and turning passive readers into loyal fans.

The real breakthrough came when we launched her first online course, the "Glowing Lean System." This program was what we offered at our merch booth—a premium offering that felt like the natural next step after someone had already connected with her story. Remember how Joshua Bell's violin performance was worth either pocket change or hundreds of dollars, depending on the context? Well, in the first 24 hours of launching the course, Kimberly generated $100,000 in revenue. It was the same knowledge she'd been sharing in private kitchens—just packaged and perceived differently.

THE COMMUNITY EFFECT

The thing about perception is that it becomes more powerful when it's shared. Think about it—when you're the only one in a subway station appreciating a violin performance, you might doubt your judgment. But when you're in a packed concert hall, surrounded by others showing their appreciation, your perception of the performance's value is reinforced.

We created this same effect for Kimberly by building what we called her "Community of Beauties." It started as a simple Facebook group for her book readers, but then it grew into something much more powerful: a tribe of over 22,000 passionate followers. These weren't just passive readers; they were active participants in Kimberly's movement. They shared their transformations, swapped recipes, and became living testimonials of her methods.

To understand how powerful this was, let me tell you about our "glowing green smoothie challenge." Instead of Kimberly trying to convince people one by one that her methods worked (like playing violin for individual commuters), we created a two-week challenge where thousands of people would try her signature smoothie recipe together. Each participant had to share photos of themselves drinking the smoothie on day one and day 14.

What happened next was magical. As people started seeing real results—better skin, more energy, weight loss—they became evangelical about Kimberly's methods. Their before-and-after photos and success stories weren't just testimonials; they became part of Kimberly's growing symphony. Each transformation added a new note. Each success story enriched the melody. The community wasn't just consuming content—they were co-creating the experience, building something far more powerful than any single voice could achieve. Their shared journeys and collective wins created a wave of social proof that no amount of traditional marketing could match. It was like turning individual subway listeners into an entire concert hall of devoted fans, not just watching the performance but becoming part of the orchestra itself, each one amplifying the perception of Kimberly's expertise.

The results were crazy. I helped her blog go from 30,000 monthly visitors to over 500,000 monthly visitors. She landed three *New York Times* bestsellers. She launched successful product lines, from probiotics to yoga programs. Her email list grew to over 100,000 subscribers. Her company generated millions of dollars in yearly revenue. Most importantly, she was now reaching people in over 200 countries, transforming lives at a scale that would have been impossible in her one-on-one business model.

Just like how Joshua Bell's music didn't change between the subway and the concert hall, Kimberly's knowledge and expertise remained the same. What changed was the context—the way her expertise was presented, packaged, and perceived by the world.

PERCEPTION CREATES REALITY

Here's what we can learn from both Joshua Bell's subway experiment and Kimberly's transformation. Talent alone isn't enough. Expertise alone isn't enough. Even working with A-list celebrities isn't enough. What matters is creating the right context for your value to be properly perceived.

In today's digital world, this means building your own "online concert hall"—a brand ecosystem that positions you as the authority you truly are. Your website becomes your stage. Your content becomes your performance. Your social media channels become your orchestra sections, each playing its part in the larger symphony of your brand. And your community becomes your audience, not just listening but actively participating in your success story.

But here's the most powerful part—unlike a physical concert hall, which can only hold so many people, your digital presence can reach millions. It works for you 24/7, across every time zone. While Kimberly was sleeping, someone in Australia could be watching her course videos. While she was working with one client, thousands could be reading her blog posts or trying her recipes.

Because of the evergreen nature of the digital world, perception influences people who have never met you before. This is why the power of perception actually creates your reality. It isn't an artificial, vanity metric; it's a real business superpower.

Perception is why people want to be at the top of search engines. It's the reason why there is so much talk about going viral. The more people who see you and your message, the more opportunities you will have to influence your followers. Today, consumers are educated—they have been trained to look for social proof, whether that's through testimonials, review sites, or just word of mouth. Perception is what shapes a customer's excitement to share your brand with their friends.

This is the true power of perception in the digital age. It's not about pretending to be something you're not. It's about creating the right environment for your genuine expertise to shine. Just as Joshua Bell needed the proper venue and atmosphere for his talent to be truly appreciated, you need the right digital infrastructure for your knowledge to reach its full potential.

Remember, we're all playing our own kind of music. As I said in the introduction, mastering social media is a game. The real question is: Are you performing in a subway station, hoping someone notices? Or have you committed to building your own concert hall, where your audience shows up ready to listen, trust, and buy?

Chapter 6

THE CELEBRITY GURU PHENOMENON

Those who follow the crowd usually get lost in it.

—Anonymous

As I shared in the author's note for this book, the connotation behind the word "influencer" has shifted in recent years. By now, you've probably caught on that I have bigger aspirations for you than to just be another cookie-cutter influencer. But in order to know where you're going, I think it's invaluable to examine the past to see where you've been. In our current day and age of 24-hour news cycles and being "chronically online," it can feel a little like Ferris Bueller's classic quote: "Life moves pretty fast. If you don't stop and look around once in a while, you could miss it." There is no greater example of that than the rapid progression and evolution of the term "influencer." But to understand that, we first need to time-travel.

The influencer industry is still pretty new. In the future, historians might judge what phase we're in now, but I'll propose my view of it as an industry professional. I think we're well past the infancy stage. In fact, the influencer industry has already spent a fair amount of time in the "toddler" stage. Like toddlers, we ran around this new exciting world screaming and going wild. We tested out every approach, metaphorically poking our fingers into electric sockets to see if it would be a good idea. In true toddler fashion, we did some seriously annoying things, but every now and then, we did something smart (almost always purely by accident). My view is that we're now in the kind of "older kid" phase. We've calmed down; we've had our fun. The industry is mature enough to start having more grown-up conversations and apply more grown-up logic and reasoning. So, with this in mind, I think it's worthwhile to start doing just that. In this section of the book, we're going to take a look at the story of how we got here, and try to surmise the "why" of it all. If you're going to be playing this career game yourself, it's of great value to start with a solid foundational understanding of the industry you're in or want to be in.

We live in the Influencer Age. If you're reading this book, you probably either are an expert building an online presence already or hope to become one. A recent survey revealed that a staggering 86% of young Americans (between ages 13 and 38) want to become social media influencers.

It's not rocket science to see why everyone wants to become an influencer. Our heroes used to be Hollywood A-listers, rock stars, and athletes. Now our heroes are influencers. Influencers are the new celebrities. Near my office in Hollywood, there are tons of influencers filming content for TikTok and Instagram daily. That's not to say that Hollywood A-listers, rock stars, and athletes have disappeared. But guess what? Each one of them is playing the influencer game too.

Wherever you are on your professional journey, your job as an expert building your brand is to facilitate a relationship between your brand and your audience. The million-dollar question I'll answer in this book is: How do you turn that dream into reality?

LEARNING BUSINESS WITH THE KARDASHIANS

Many of us, when we look back on our lives, realize that the career paths we ended up choosing were so often the result of a seed that was planted in our childhood or teenage years. When we graduate from high school, we're faced with one of the biggest choices in our lives: What career are we going to pursue? Whether we're deciding on what college course to sign up for or what business to start working in, we've got to make a choice from a list of overwhelmingly endless options. It's rare that we make this choice completely randomly. For many of us, we choose a specific path because we've had some kind of advantageous start in that area already. Maybe you loved playing with Lego, and over the years you moved up from building a 10-piece house to a Lego® *Star Wars*™ 75192 Millennium Falcon. This gave you experience with "engineering thinking." So maybe you decide to study mechanical engineering at college. Or maybe you were in the school play, and you've already learned some skills about projecting your voice, memorizing lines, and using a lot of theater jargon, like which side is "stage right." So you might think it's a good idea to pursue an acting career.

Sometimes it's not necessarily a technical advantage that you have. Sometimes it's because you've spent many hours experiencing life in that professional world. This may have been before your time, but in the '80s, one of the most popular TV shows was a courtroom drama called *L.A. Law*. This factoid isn't too amazing on its own, but when you see the cultural repercussions, the impact is fascinating. About a decade after the show aired, a college did a survey among its freshman law students. Eighty-three percent of the students noted that, as young teenagers, *L.A.*

Law was their favorite TV show. Such a high statistic is unlikely to be a random coincidence.

In previous generations, the world of business was totally separated from children. Apart from "kid business ventures" like setting up a sidewalk lemonade stand with a cute handwritten sign, or perhaps flipping baseball cards in the schoolyard, education on business matters generally started in college. If you saw a kid walking around the "business and marketing" section of a bookstore, you would be pretty safe to assume that they're lost and looking for their mom. However, many Gen Z kids started their business studies in their early teens, some even earlier. Most spent at least four to six hours a week attending courses. Many attended at least one course every single day (including Saturdays and Sundays). These courses started out as 22 minutes each, but the demand and hunger for more and more commerce knowledge resulted in the lessons being extended to 46 minutes each. The teachers that educated these diligent young students were far from any ordinary business faculty professor. In fact, in some ways they were beyond Ivy League university status. They were the real deal, and they were giving not just a class but a master class.

AJ? Dude? What on earth are you talking about? What college was this? I'll tell you, but don't laugh. At least, not until you've read my explanation.

The business college that many Gen Z students attended was the Kardashian College. Or, to keep with the Kardashian style, *Kardashian Kollege.*

The Kardashians were the pioneers of the social media influencer industry. In many ways, they single-handedly invented the concept and perfected the business model. The timing of this collided with another modern trend, and the combined result massively affected, inspired, and educated an entire generation. The trend that it collided with was reality TV.

Hundreds and millions of people from around the planet watched every single second of the Kardashian family's life. For hours and hours, over years and years. We envied their luxurious lifestyles, copied their outfits and hairstyles, got involved with their petty sibling dramas, gossiped about their romantic relationships . . . but those were all the little sparkly things around what we were really watching and admiring. What the show was really about was a family building a business empire and experimenting with a new business model concept. It was a true first-time-in-history opportunity. The Kardashians' unique business model was not only totally nuts—it turned out to be totally genius. It was because they had understood the zeitgeist, the cultural climate of the era. And they realized what it was before any of us did. That was their first-to-market advantage. While the Kardashians may have started out as token influencers, today they are thought leaders in their respective fields—titans of industry, as they say.

Kim Kardashian is much more than just a powerhouse media personality. Her brand Skims is worth nearly $4 billion! Her reality show start garnered her massive attention, and she has been able to leverage that into massive influence. But here's what most people miss about the Kardashians' success: They expertly leveraged their flagship programming. *Keeping Up with the Kardashians* wasn't just a reality show—it was the central, consistent show that anchored their personal brand and allowed them to expand into countless ventures. Each episode followed recognizable formats: family drama, business meetings, relationship updates. Viewers knew exactly what to expect, and that predictability created appointment television. Kim's social media follows the same principle. Her "day in the life" posts, her Skims campaigns, her family moments—these aren't random content. They're recurring content series that people anticipate. She's not just posting; she's programming her personal media company.

DESIGNING INFLUENCE

Coco Chanel, the founder of luxury powerhouse Chanel, was the first fashion designer to be a public "influencer" figure. Prior to Ms. Chanel, fashion houses were not associated with public persona like they are today. They were businesses with factories, and the public simply knew the name of the manufacturer. But Coco Chanel presented *herself* as a persona that represented what *her* brand was all about. She was regularly in the public eye, and she was admired for her personal style. She used her fame and public platform to influence a generation of young Parisian women in matters of fashion, as well as general lifestyle advice beyond clothing. Sound familiar?

To a large extent, Coco Chanel pioneered the first edition of the influencer model. She was outspoken and controversial about her daring opinions (like introducing the shocking concept of women being allowed to wear pants); she challenged the status quo and made bold statements (such as saying that she preferred women in makeup); she generated notoriety through controversy (regularly dissing other fashion designers and refusing to dress royalty); and her life was filled with romantic intrigue and gossip-worthy drama (from dating royalty to poets, having dalliances with sugar daddies, and even refusing a marriage proposal from the Duke of Westminster).

She was an early example of what I call a guru. Her specialty was that she was the best talent in the fashion industry. Chanel understood something important that today's creators often miss: She chose her own typecasting. Instead of letting others define her, she intentionally positioned herself as the rebellious fashion revolutionary. Every controversial statement, every bold design choice reinforced this character she'd created. She wasn't trying to be everything to everyone—she owned her specific category and dominated it completely. Besides her hard skills, she was also a specialist in the fashion of lifestyle. Her audience had a deep respect for her as the expert, so her words held great value. Whatever advice she gave, millions of French women and girls would follow.

Fast-forward again closer to the Kardashian timeline, and we arrive at that strange and wonderful time known as the '90s and early 2000s, when the thought leader model was really refined. For most of us growing up, we looked for knowledge and answers to life's biggest questions on the television. There were three superhero women who dominated television: Oprah Winfrey, Martha Stewart, and Ellen DeGeneres. Each of these women mastered what I call "lifestyle authority"—combining expertise, entertainment, and commerce in ways that would later become the blueprint for social media influencers to follow. Rather than just hocking products and garnering sales, these women began offering lifestyle advice that made a difference in their audiences' lives. They became touted as more than just talking heads entertaining a crowd; they became relatable experts who shared their wisdom with the world.

Let's face it, no one is more iconic than Oprah. Oprah pioneered the art of authentic connection with a mass audience while building a massive media empire that dominated television. She had the Midas touch when it came to recommending resources for her audience. If Oprah bestowed a blessing upon your book, product, or service, you were instantly catapulted into stardom. Like a booster rocket taking off with the Oprah starship, you were now breaking through the stratosphere. This became affectionately known as the "Oprah effect." This phenomenon is now called "influencer marketing," and Oprah was one of the forerunners.

Oprah and the women who came before her paved the way for other women such as Martha Stewart to develop their own lifestyle brands in the early 2000s. Martha was also much more than an influencer; she was a thought leader whose brand transcended mere lifestyle advice. It embodied a philosophy of living well, deeply rooted in the idea that beauty, order, and creativity can heal and elevate our lives. As you may expect, this message was powerful. Martha Stewart took homemaking and elevated it into an aspirational lifestyle brand. She followed in the footsteps of people like Julia Child and Martha Graham, who built their own personality-driven media brands. She became famous for showing viewers that anyone could turn practical expertise (cooking, decorating, gardening) into a multiplatform business empire. Her magazines, TV shows, and product lines created a complete Martha Stewart universe that fans could buy into. Again, she was a trendsetter for what today's current influencers are doing when they create their own branded worlds. Through her books, TV shows, and products, Martha Stewart inspired people to transform the ordinary into the extraordinary. She became a star because she took the mundane aspects of everyday domestic life—cooking a meal, setting a table, or growing a garden—and transformed them into something transcendental by teaching how these simple everyday tasks can become healing, meditative daily acts of self-love and enthusiasm for living a better life.

Ellen DeGeneres arrived on the precipice of major cultural change. Her queer identity ushered in a new sense of belonging and acceptance for audiences who had been marginalized by lack of representation in previous television generations. Ellen brought humor, dancing, and incredible impromptu banter between her and her guests that made audiences rave about her. This helped her become likable on a wide scale, showing how personality-driven content could create deep audience connections. Her famous selfie at the 2014 Oscars (which briefly "broke Twitter") was perhaps the perfect bridge between old and new media—a talk show host using social media to create a viral moment that cemented her legacy as a thought leader. When she spoke, people listened.

At the turn of the millennium, people like Martha Stewart, Oprah Winfrey, and Ellen DeGeneres weren't just influencing, they were instructing. They showed their audiences how to live, what to value, and how to aspire. Monkey see, monkey do. Humans learn by watching others demonstrate, and these women mastered that on a global stage. They didn't just play the media game; they redefined it. Oprah didn't just host her talk show; she built Harpo Productions, the *O* magazine, and the Oprah Winfrey Network around her signature show. Martha Stewart didn't just give lifestyle tips; she launched Martha Stewart Living Omnimedia, anchored by her signature show, *Martha Stewart Living.* They understood that their names weren't just brands. They were personal media companies—with multiple content channels reinforcing a singular identity. What's wild is that the strategies they used to dominate old media . . . are now the same strategies creators are using to win in the new media world—just with different tools. Instead of TV networks, it's YouTube. Instead of print magazines, it's newsletters and blogs. But the playbook is the same: Create consistent shows across multiple touchpoints—and become the channel people tune into.

So you're now up to speed with how you and the rest of humanity got here. Human history has been divided into many ages: the Stone Age, the Bronze Age, the Iron Age, and so on. You'll note that each age is defined by the revolutionary tool, material, or technology that made for a new world of opportunities—a new ecosystem and an evolved way of life. You, dear reader, are a pioneer in the Social Media Age. Social media and emergent AI technologies are the tools that will be shaping our evolution as a species.

As you're well aware, everyone in the world today (children included), without much skill or experience or budget, can create professional-looking photographs, build complex websites, shoot and edit video in cinema quality with expert-level effects, and work on just about any other creative pursuit. You, I, and everyone else on the internet can create whatever we can dream of and share it with the world, just like Paris Hilton did. We are living in a time where the celebrity dream is open to every human. Today, it is you versus every other human on the planet. Every human has access to the same platforms and tools. Every digital agency offers a relatively similar service and strategy. This should make you pause and think.

What can we take away from the story of how our society learned to set its sights on becoming influencers, thanks to our forerunners: the Kardashians, Paris Hilton, Coco Chanel, Oprah, Martha Stewart, and Ellen DeGeneres?

You're by no means unique in your dream of becoming a limitless creator. You've been conditioned to go in this direction through pop culture since you were a kid. But if you want to stand out, remember that true influence isn't about simply chasing followers; it's about building a legacy as a thought leader by combining authenticity, expertise, and smart branding.

While at first blush it may look like there's a big difference between Ellen DeGeneres and Kim K, all these businesses have something in common—even the Kardashians. *They focus on serving their audiences by providing them with answers to their most pressing problems through their own personal mastery. But in order to do that, they all had to focus on creating a well-positioned, personality-driven brand.*

Chapter 7

BUILDING YOUR PERSONAL GURU BRAND

> Every block of stone has a statue inside it, and it is the
> task of the sculptor to discover it.
>
> —Michelangelo

There's a quote I often come back to when I think about the Guru's Journey and what it really means to be a leader in your space. It comes from the movie *Catch Me If You Can*, where the main character, Frank Abagnale Jr., manages to convince an entire hospital staff that he's a doctor. When asked how he pulled it off, his response was striking in its simplicity: He just stayed one chapter ahead in the medical textbook. That line stuck with me—not because it's about deception, but because it reveals a deeper truth about perception and influence. You don't have to be the best in the world to start. You don't need the most credentials or the loudest voice. You just need to be one chapter ahead of the people you want to help, and have the clarity and confidence to share what you know. That's all it takes.

This is something most aspiring gurus miss. They wait until they feel "ready," until they've mastered everything, until they've earned every certification, before putting themselves out there. But transformation—the kind that truly moves people—doesn't come from having all the answers. It comes from lived experience. From going through something yourself, learning from it, and being willing to guide others through that same process. When I first started helping Kimberly Snyder build her brand, she wasn't necessarily known as the most academically credentialed nutritionist in the world, but she had something more valuable. She had lived through her own health transformation and developed a unique, highly effective approach that actually worked. She was steps ahead of the millions of people struggling with the same issues she had faced, because she'd walked that path herself. If you want to build a meaningful personal brand—one that positions you as the Oprah, Martha Stewart, or Mike Ferry of your niche—you must understand this: It's not about being the smartest person in the room. It's about being the person who has been there, who gets it, and who shows others what's possible. That's what makes you trustworthy. That's what makes you real.

Things have changed. We live in a world where attention is the most valuable currency, and in this world, expertise alone no longer guarantees success. Every day we see brilliant people remain invisible while others, with only a fraction of their knowledge, attract huge audiences and build thriving businesses. Why does that happen? Because they understand something most experts don't. They understand that positioning matters more than perfection. And while some people still think that successful personal brands are built on talent, charisma, or luck, the reality is different. Guru brands are not born. They're built, one strategic move at a time, by people who understand how to shape perception, create connection, and lead with purpose.

What do I mean by "built"? I mean that this is not something you throw together overnight. Building real influence isn't about chasing trends or hoping stuff goes viral. It's about understanding this is a process that takes time. It's a game with structure, patterns, and specific challenges that you'll need to navigate. There are goals you're aiming for, actions you'll need to repeat consistently, and obstacles that will try to pull you off course. Your job is to become the person people think of when they need help. And in order to do that, there are three core strategies that every successful guru figures out.

But here's the good news: You don't need anyone to give you permission to start. You don't need to wait to be picked or validated. The gatekeepers are gone. You already have what it takes, especially if you're willing to step forward and lead from what you've lived. If you've made it even one step beyond where your audience is now, you're qualified to lead them. And sometimes, that's all people need. Someone just one chapter ahead.

THE LENS PRINCIPLE

If you've ever found yourself captivated by a certain thought leader on social media or TV, it's probably not just because of what they're talking about—it's because of *how* they talk about it. The most influential people in any industry don't just repeat information. They filter it through a deeply personal lens that comes from lived experience, inner clarity, and years of grappling with real-world problems. This unique way of seeing things becomes their secret weapon. It's what makes people actually listen to them instead of scrolling past. They don't just teach—they reveal. And in a world where most content sounds like a slightly altered version of someone else's script, that kind of clarity cuts through the noise.

One of the most valuable lessons I picked up from social media strategist Kallaway was the importance of perspective. Most experts rely on familiar templates or trending topics, which can be useful, but without a unique lens, the content feels repetitive instead of remarkable. The problem is, when your content looks and sounds just like everyone else's, it blends into the background. It doesn't matter how good your advice is—if the perspective behind it is generic, it becomes forgettable. The human brain is wired to notice what feels fresh, what disrupts patterns, and what introduces novelty. That's why shows like *Hot Ones* took off. On paper, it's just another interview format. But the twist—watching celebrities eat painfully spicy wings while answering deep questions—makes it impossible not to click. It's different enough to trigger curiosity, but still familiar enough to understand instantly. That's the power of a well-defined lens. It turns ordinary content into something memorable.

Understanding this also gives you an edge when it comes to virality. People don't just share content to be helpful. They share it to signal something about themselves. When someone reposts your video, forwards your blog, or quotes your ideas, they're not just giving you visibility—they're using your content as a way to earn social credibility. It's a form of currency. The more your content elevates their status, the more likely they are to pass it along. That means your job isn't just to educate. It's to make your ideas feel worth sharing. To do that, you need to make people feel like they're seeing something in a new way.

There are only a few combinations of content that actually work when it comes to generating this kind of traction. The first one—common idea with a common point of view—is what most people default to. It's safe, predictable, and easily lost in the feed. Unless you're the very first to post about a trending topic, this kind of content rarely spreads. Then there's the path that most successful gurus take: common idea, uncommon point of view. This is when you talk about something familiar, but through a lens that feels fresh. Oprah didn't invent talk shows, but she brought radical empathy and personal transformation to the format. That shift in lens changed everything.

Another powerful angle is an uncommon idea with a common point of view. Tim Ferriss is a great example of this. His ideas—early retirement, digital nomadism, body hacking—were considered strange when they first appeared. But he delivered them through a framework that felt structured, logical, and grounded in efficiency. The concepts were unusual, but the delivery made them easy to digest. That's what made his ideas spread.

The final combination—an uncommon idea paired with an uncommon point of view—is the one that struggles the most to gain mainstream traction. When both the idea itself and the way it's being communicated are unfamiliar, people don't know how to engage with it. There's no hook, no mental reference point, no easy way to understand what's being said or why it matters. It becomes too abstract, too alienating, and too easy to ignore. This is exactly what happened with blockchain and Bitcoin in their early years. The idea was revolutionary, but the way it was being explained—through technical language, cryptographic jargon, and libertarian futurist ideals—felt inaccessible to the average person. Most people didn't understand it, and so they didn't trust it. It wasn't until more grounded narratives emerged, like the idea of decentralizing finance, giving power back to the people, or using blockchain for real-world applications, that mainstream adoption began to take root. The concept didn't change, but the way it was positioned did. The same idea, now paired with a more relatable lens, suddenly made sense.

That's why your lens matters so much. It's the one thing no one else can copy. It comes from your story, your challenges, and the unique ways you've solved problems. And it's not something you can rush or force. It develops naturally when you've truly lived what you're teaching. People can feel that. They can sense when your insights come from personal clarity versus borrowed language. In a world overflowing with content, what sets you apart is not just what you know—it's the way you've come to know it.

THE THREE STRATEGIC MOVES

Now that you understand the foundation that gurus are built through the strategic combination of lived experience and intentional positioning, let's take things one level deeper. The gurus who win consistently don't just rely on insight. They follow a repeatable set of moves. These moves aren't flashy or mysterious, but they are powerful. They give you structure in a world that often feels chaotic and unpredictable, and they help you rise above the noise while others burn out chasing every trend. If you want to build a guru brand that lasts, there are Three Strategic Moves that must become part of your foundation.

Move 1: Own Your Category

One of the most essential things every successful guru has done is simple in theory, but rare in execution: They chose their label before anyone else could assign one to them. Whether they did it consciously or instinctively, they decided who they wanted to be, what they wanted to be known for, and how they would frame their work in the mind of the audience. They became the cause, not the effect. Instead of reacting to how others perceived them, they took control of the narrative and shaped their brand with intention.

But here's the key insight most people miss: You're not just positioning expertise, you're creating a character. Bill Nye isn't just a science educator; he's Bill Nye the Science Guy, a specific persona who makes science accessible and fun. The sharks on *Shark Tank* aren't just investors; they're distinct characters with recognizable personalities. Your job is to become a character too—a heightened, intentional version of yourself that consistently demonstrates high value. Erika Kullberg didn't just become "a lawyer who makes content." She became "the lawyer who reads the fine print so you don't have to." That's character work. When you show up as the same recognizable persona every time, you become impossible to ignore.

This act of authorship is more than personal branding. It's positioning your unique character to claim your category before the market chooses it for you. The human brain is wired to categorize. Your audience is going to put you in a mental box whether you like it or not. The only question is: Will that box reflect who you really are and the value you provide, or will it be a random label based on surface-level impressions? Most content creators don't realize this is happening. They post a few things, go with the flow, and suddenly find themselves typecast as "the guy who skateboarded with juice" or "the girl who does trending dance routines." But the most iconic personal brands are intentional. They choose their category early and reinforce it consistently until there's no confusion about who they are or what they stand for.

Look at Alex Hormozi. He didn't start as a mainstream business guru. He began in a specific, narrow lane: gym owners. His brand, his books, and his offers were all targeted at helping gym owners grow through better sales systems. But here's where he made a genius move. He claimed that niche fully before expanding. Once he dominated that category, he transitioned upstream. Instead of just being "the gym guy," he reframed himself as the guy who helps businesses make more money through offers and operations. Today, he owns an entirely new, more expansive category: helping entrepreneurs scale their businesses with clarity and discipline. He didn't wait to be invited into the broader business world. He expanded his category with intention and then brought the audience with him.

Owning your category doesn't mean locking yourself into a box. It means choosing a foundation that combines three things: your core skill set, the real needs of your audience, and the intersection of your personal interests with a gap in the market. You begin with a tight niche, one that matches your natural strength, and you expand from there as your authority grows. If you try to be everything to everyone, you dilute your signal and get ignored. But when you pick one thing and master it, you give people a reason to pay attention. This is how you build identity in the new media game. Instead of being another voice in the crowd, you become known for something specific. That recognition becomes trust. And trust becomes leverage for bigger opportunities.

Move 2: Create Your Method

The second move every guru must master is turning their expertise into a method. Not just ideas or insights, but a structured, repeatable system that leads people toward a transformation. This is what separates a content creator from a true authority. It's not about how much you know. It's about how clearly you can show others a path from where they are now to where they want to be.

Your method is how your ideas become real in other people's lives. It doesn't have to be groundbreaking. It just needs to be proven, teachable, and rooted in your experience. When it's done right, it becomes more than just a framework—it becomes your intellectual property. A method gives your brand structure. It becomes the thing people refer to, pass around, and remember. Think of Tony Robbins and his 6 Human Needs. Think of James Clear and *Atomic Habits*. Think of Mike Ferry and the Mike Ferry system. These are not just concepts; rather, they're systems that deliver transformation, and they're owned by the people who created them.

Whether your transformation is delivered through a teaching framework, a coaching system, a physical product, or even a piece of software, the principle is the same. Your method is the repeatable delivery of a promise. It's the structured way your value gets applied in someone's life. It can be a set of habits like Stephen Covey's *7 Habits of Highly Effective People*, or it can be a meal plan, a digital tool, a coaching curriculum, or a product line sold in stores—like what Martha Stewart did with her

Kmart collections. Martha took her lifestyle philosophy and translated it into accessible, tangible tools that allowed everyday people to feel like they were bringing elegance, order, and creativity into their homes. The method wasn't just in the content of her TV shows or books. It lived inside the sheets, the kitchenware, the towels, and the storage bins that carried her brand into people's lives. What matters most is that your method creates consistent results and can scale beyond you. When your ideas are packaged in a way that others can use over and over again, you move from being a one-to-one guide to becoming the creator of a transformational system. And that's what allows your brand to grow in both influence and impact.

THE SKIMS TRANSFORMATION METHOD

Kim Kardashian didn't just launch another shapewear brand. She built Skims as a transformation method, embedded into a product. Her vision was to create garments that helped people feel more confident in their bodies, not just look slimmer. She solved for body diversity, comfort, and inclusivity in ways the market hadn't seen before, offering a wide range of sizes and skin-tone shades that were often ignored by traditional brands. The transformation was instant and physical, but also emotional. And because Skims was productized, it could scale. This created impact and identity at the same time. That's what made it more than clothing. It became a method.

Whether your transformation is delivered through a digital product, a live program, a physical brand, or a signature piece of content, the principle is the same. Your method should be rooted in something you've lived, something you've tested, and something others can use to achieve real results. When you package your value into a repeatable system, you stop trading time for attention and start building something scalable. And that's how movements are born.

Move 3: Build Your Programming

Now we move from positioning and packaging into execution. This is how you actually show up, share your value, and build the infrastructure of a brand that people trust. Most experts think content is just about posting. But gurus think about programming. They understand that their presence isn't random. It's rhythmic. It's intentional. It's consistent enough to be recognized, but dynamic enough to keep evolving.

Programming is how your method gets distributed across every channel you show up on. It's your weekly podcast, daily short-form clips, long-form YouTube videos, newsletters, events, products, digital courses, and emails. It's not just content. It's your brand operating like a media company. The experts who win long-term treat their platforms that way. They build content systems their audience begins to recognize, remember, and return to. One of the most effective ways to do that is through a social-first show—a repeatable content series designed specifically for social media platforms, where the format, pacing, visuals, and storytelling are optimized first and foremost for native performance, discovery, and engagement on those platforms. The show becomes uniquely yours through your tone, delivery, and point of view. It could be a podcast, short-form videos on Instagram or TikTok, or a long-form video on YouTube. What matters is that it's structured, familiar, and emotionally consistent. Over time, your audience starts to associate the rhythm, the visuals, and even the vibe with you. They know what to expect, and they come back for it. Your social-first show doesn't just deliver information. It builds identity. It anchors your brand. This isn't about chasing trends. It's about building trust through structure. When your programming is intentional, your entire brand ecosystem feels connected. That consistency builds trust. That trust turns followers into fans—and those fans into clients, customers, and loyal believers.

Look at how top creators today use their social-first shows across every format. Jay Shetty doesn't just post reels; he runs a podcast, writes books, sends newsletters, and hosts live events that all reinforce the same voice and values of his personal brand. MrBeast treats every upload like a primetime special, combining spectacle with structure. Mel Robbins consistently leverages her core methods like the 5 Second Rule and her "Let Them" theory across her popular podcast, books, and daily social media content. And before the rise of social media, Oprah's daytime show and *Martha Stewart Living* were perfect examples of TV show programming. They created recurring content that shaped how millions of people saw them and built empires around their identity. None of these content creators operate randomly. Their shows allow them to stay relevant, scale their impact, and grow businesses without constantly trading time for content.

When you build your programming correctly, you start to create a feeling across every channel. Whether someone is watching a video, listening to a podcast, reading an email, or buying your product, it all feels like it came from the same world. That's how trust compounds. And that's what turns a scattered online presence into a real brand. Your goal isn't just visibility. It's depth. It's consistency. It's coherence. This is how you make strategic moves in the attention game. Instead of random posts hoping for luck, you're building a system that consistently delivers value and builds trust. You want people to recognize your tone, your values, your energy, and your message no matter what platform they're on. That's when your audience stops browsing and starts belonging. They feel like they've entered your orbit—and once they're in, they don't want to leave. This is how you shift from playing defense on social media to owning mindshare. You stop chasing the algorithm. You start shaping perception. And when your positioning, your method, and your programming all work together, you don't just get noticed. You become unforgettable.

EMMA CHAMBERLAIN: FROM VLOGS TO MEDIA EMPIRE

Emma Chamberlain started with low-budget YouTube vlogs that felt raw, chaotic, and deeply personal. But beneath the messiness was a repeatable format that became her social-first show. Her lifestyle vlog, with its distinct editing, self-aware humor, and unfiltered voice, became the content that built her brand. Viewers didn't just watch—they returned for that specific feeling. That consistency became the foundation of her programming. She expanded into a podcast, *anything goes*, which carried the same intimate tone. Her product line, Chamberlain Coffee, reflected the same aesthetic and attitude. Even her partnerships with brands like Louis Vuitton weren't random. They aligned with the identity she had shaped through years of consistent story-telling. What started as a social-first show on her YouTube channel became a full brand ecosystem, reaching tens of millions and fueling a business that extended across media, products, and global fashion. What looked casual was actually a system that turned content into connection, and connection into a cultural brand.

THE LONG GAME

Here's where these three moves become powerful: when they work together as an integrated system. Your category gives you a clear lane to dominate. Your method gives you something unique to teach within that category. Your programming gives you a consistent way to deliver that method to your audience. When all three elements align, you stop being just another voice in the noise and start becoming the voice that people seek out for guidance in your specific area of expertise. This is how positioning compounds into authority. Every piece of content reinforces who you are, what you teach, and why people should trust you. Over time, this consistency builds the kind of influence that transcends individual posts or viral moments.

Most experts approach social media with a short-term mindset. They want immediate results, instant recognition, and quick wins. But gurus understand something different: They're building for tomorrow's authority, not today's metrics. This long-term perspective changes everything. Instead of chasing trends, you focus on timeless principles. Instead of optimizing for likes, you optimize for trust. Instead of trying to please everyone, you focus on serving your specific audience exceptionally well. The beautiful thing about playing the long game is that most of your competition won't. They'll get distracted by shiny objects, chase whatever's trending, or give up when they don't see immediate results. As Alex Hormozi says, "Entrepreneurship isn't a game of best man wins. It's a game of last man standing."[6] This gives you a massive advantage if you're willing to trust the process. But playing the long game effectively requires more than just persistence. You need to understand how authority actually develops, how attention really works in the digital economy, and how to build systems that compound your efforts over time. That's exactly what we'll explore in the chapters ahead—because understanding how to position yourself as a guru is just the beginning. The real game is learning how to systematically build the influence, attention, and business success that makes that positioning sustainable.

Chapter 8

THE GURU LADDER

You get a car! *You* get a car. *Everybody* gets a car!

—Oprah Winfrey

Each time the talk show host pointed at a new person, she was instantly changing their lives. In the span of under a minute, she had changed the life of every person in her audience that day. She was simply that powerful.

Literally at the snap of her fingers, she could transform hundreds of realities, all while filming one of the most beloved television talk shows of all time. She knew what she was doing when she handed out the keys to brand-new cars to everyone in the audience that day. More than just helping them financially, she was ushering in a new paradigm of collective hope. Here was a celebrity who, instead of shaming people out of poverty, was actively giving back to her community of fans. This sent a ripple out into the collective and, through courageous acts of generosity, made her one of the wealthiest people on the planet.

Of course, you know who I'm talking about, don't you? She's so famous for being wise, generous, and charismatic that she only goes by her first name. Just five letters that spell major top-of-the-charts level celebrity: O-P-R-A-H.

The situation I just described above is the aforementioned "Oprah effect" in full force. Oprah has a Midas touch, where literally almost anything she vouches for turns to gold. Oprah's Book Club selections are heralded as world-changing literature. Fad diets, trends, and engaging social conversations discussed by Oprah quickly reverberate around the globe to be embraced by the masses. Thanks to her high-level guru positioning, her influence extends far beyond that of a normal TV show host. In biblical texts, Jesus was said to have turned water into wine. Oprah, as the embodiment of a thought leader who has truly achieved legendary guru status, can turn *attention into dollars*, all while making her followers feel better about themselves and their journeys through life.

Oprah and her team were immaculately well organized in making sure that she strategically appeared with other guru-level celebrities to ensure that her brand always garnered favorable associations—the backbone of any good positioning strategy. She also was careful about any strategic partnerships and limited how much media exposure she received. These subtle tactics were an artform that helped her create an incredible personal brand that almost everyone on the planet can be envious of.

The good news is that you can adopt the same principles that she did and apply them to your own personal brand.

AUTHORITATIVE POSITIONING MEETS PUBLIC PERCEPTION

Oprah and her producers saw that other talk shows focused on highly charged negative storylines in which dissenting voices were the predominant form of entertainment. Oprah shifted that narrative and flipped it on its head by focusing on positive stories that left her audience feeling uplifted and inspired. Taking control of the creative reins driving her brand helped her navigate her meteoric rise to fame, all while doing things on her terms. By 2011, after 25 years of broadcasting, her TV show *The Oprah Winfrey Show* was earning $6 million a week—that's over $300 million per year! One of the major reasons for her success was her discernment in branching out into new avenues to expand the brand beyond what it was. She expanded to Oprah's Book Club, DVD sales, television, film, and production ventures, affiliate marketing partnerships, and even her own television channel, the Oprah Winfrey Network.

Even when she received negative press for expressing her opinions, fans and loyal followers of the show went to bat backing her up due to the fact that she was always honest with her audience. In the '90s when she scared her audience into not buying hamburger meat for fear of a mad cow disease breakout, sales of beef plummeted. That's the power of authoritative positioning meeting the gravitational pull of public perception!

As a billionaire, Oprah has been able to help inspire millions of people around the world, and her success has allowed her to champion her own projects based on her ethics, values, and personal beliefs. But how does someone get to the pinnacle of success like she did?

If you want to become the next mini Oprah of your niche, it's all about how people see you. That's why you want to focus on the right audience from the start. These are the people who'll actually help you grow into the guru you want to become. For instance, if you start out as a low-budget brand serving low-end consumers, it'll be very difficult to position yourself as a high-end brand in the future. Under that same logic, it might be hard for a spiritual and optimistic authority like Oprah to position herself as a raunchy late-night stand-up comedian. Even though she has the performing talent to do that, it would require her to position herself differently in the minds of her audience, which doesn't happen overnight.

Put simply, Oprah evolved from a talk show host to the leader of a media empire through consistent brand messaging, carefully controlled media exposure, a focus on authenticity and positive content, strategic business decisions, and, above all else, a strong emotional connection with her audience.

And I know you might be asking yourself, *Why all this talk about Oprah and her ways? Sure, that worked 20 years ago, but would it work today?* The answer is: YES. Look at MrBeast, the most popular YouTuber on the planet. Today, MrBeast is notorious for lighting up YouTube viewer counts like a pinball machine during a high-scoring game every time he passes out new cars to his audience. The more outrageously generous he gets, the bigger his channel grows. Contrary to what many Gen Z content creators may believe, he's not doing something new. He's a young dog doing the same tricks that Oprah became famous for.

A BUSINESS GURU'S SUPERPOWER IS TRANSFORMATION

What Oprah and others like her are uncannily good at is attracting the same type of organic positioning that spiritual gurus like Baba Ji did. That's a fancy way of saying that a guru's positioning is driven by the emotional needs of their followers, who want their guru's wisdom. People journey far and wide to go listen to a guru—my family's adventure to see Baba Ji is a prime example. For Oprah, her essence as a personality and teacher is what promotes her brands. In some ways, her brand markets itself, through her honest personal transparency and her unprecedented global recognition.

Business gurus like Mike Ferry, on the other hand, must be strategic about how they position themselves. Since business gurus tend to have followers who are more skeptical and eager to test out the competition, it's important that they create a winning strategy that uniquely positions their brand in their market. They can do this by intentionally using strategic content and generating social proof that helps them expand the public's knowledge of their brand and how it can help benefit their lives. Business gurus must leverage marketing techniques to scale influence and generate leads consistently. They build credibility through data, testimonials, and high-value offers that work hand in hand with their content creation strategy. While spiritual gurus focus on inner transformation, business gurus tend to focus on external success, such as career advancement or wealth-building. Business gurus who want to maximize their organic positioning should steal a page out of Oprah's book and find a philosophy-driven message that combines practical solutions with deeper purpose and values. Whereas a spiritual guru leaves behind a legacy through their body of work, teachings, and scriptures, a business guru's legacy is only accessible when there is adequate attention to their market positioning. In other words, it's up to the business guru to generate awareness about why their brand is still culturally relevant.

Remember the new media game we talked about in the introduction? Most experts play this game without even realizing these levels exist, so they're hitting targets they can't see. To really understand the mechanism behind how your positioning influences your perception, look no further than the Guru Ladder. The brilliance behind this system is that it illustrates a fundamental point at the heart of building authority and influence on your journey as an expert: As you climb the five levels of the Guru Ladder, your words begin to carry more weight. This growing authority translates into real influence over your audience. This is how you begin to help your audience members slowly start transforming. This superpower, the ability to help inspire real, transformative change in your followers, gets stronger with each new level.

INTRODUCING THE GURU LADDER

Since some of you weren't around in the '80s and '90s to witness Oprah Winfrey dominate daytime television, let's bring this concept into a world you're more familiar with. Oprah was the queen of old media. She built an empire through syndicated TV, publishing, and partnerships with traditional gatekeepers. But most of you aren't trying to get a network deal or launch the next O, *The Oprah Magazine*. You're building in the age of social media, short-form video, and algorithmic discovery.

To bring the Guru Ladder to life, we need a case study who didn't just master the old rules, but rewrote them for the internet. Enter Gary Vaynerchuk. Gary is the perfect example of a modern guru who started with zero followers and built his empire entirely online, so his story makes him the ideal guinea pig to study. He began at the bottom, working in his family's liquor store. He was bagging ice, stocking shelves, and studying customer behavior. But instead of staying small, he bet early on YouTube and launched *Wine Library TV*, a scrappy but effective video series that helped grow the business from $3 million to over $60 million in revenue.

That success wasn't just about wine; it was about mastering attention. Gary turned his growing visibility into leverage, launching Vayner-Media, now one of the most influential digital agencies in the world. Today, he's not just a guru—he's a guru's guru, someone other content creators, founders, and marketers study to understand how to win in this new attention economy. In studying Gary's journey, you'll see exactly how the five levels of the Guru Ladder play out in real time. You'll see how someone evolves from a generalist to a specialist to an authority, and ultimately becomes a cultural brand with gravity of their own. Gary's journey perfectly embodies the American dream and illustrates the potential of strategic content creation and audience engagement in building a successful personal brand.

Level 1: The Generalist

When you first start peddling your knowledge and insights on your own tiny slice of the internet, you will likely be trying to figure out exactly what your audience wants. To do this, you need to go general and cast a wide net on a variety of topics. The broader your subject matter, the easier it will be to gauge audience interest and incorporate their feedback into your creative approach.

Since the generalist is in the earliest stages of influence, it's not uncommon for their advice to be a little generic. The generalist is good at parroting what other leading influencers in their industry are also saying. In some ways, they are just another voice in the crowd. A generalist has a broad knowledge base but lacks deep expertise, which means their content doesn't have a unique style yet.

At this stage of the Guru's Journey, you're still discovering your unique value. The generalist level is the jack-of-all-trades, much like Gary Vee in his early days, when he was selling baseball cards, creating lemonade stands, or experimenting with garage-sale flipping. He didn't have a specific niche yet, but as a generalist, he was gathering a wide range of skills and valuable experience. This is where everyone starts; it is inescapable. But it isn't set in stone. You can grow and evolve if you commit yourself to learning.

At this stage, you need to ask yourself, "What am I really passionate about?"

THE TAKEAWAY

You're still discovering your unique value. Your advice blends in with everyone else's because you haven't yet identified what makes your perspective special or different.

Level 2: The Specialist

Over time, with much care and practice, the generalist grows their knowledge base and sharpens their ability. Eventually, they develop some level of expertise in certain aspects of their industry. They get better at their craft, and they improve at sharing their message with their target audience.

After spending some time in the generalist phase, the specialist has figured out what everyone else is doing right and wrong. This helps them start walking the labyrinth of learning and recognizing their own strengths and weaknesses, which can be a difficult skill to master. This level of insight and self-awareness is called conscious competency, and it is the beginning of the pathway to true mastery.

At this stage, a person's natural passion rises to the surface with great speed and intensity, like a booster rocket taking off into the stratosphere. The specialist knows that to keep up with the hustle and grind of being an expert, they will have to love what they do and dedicate their lives to the pursuit of progress. To make it worth their time, they naturally gravitate toward their preferences.

This phase of the Guru's Journey is where passion meets focus. This natural desire is the spark that allows a generalist to evolve and level up to the role of a specialist. Their passion allows them to focus their time, energy, and talent on doing things they truly love, and study subjects and niche topics that make them feel alive. Doing so makes them even better at what they do.

Don't get me wrong, the specialist is still not a master—not yet, anyway. But they are clearly on the path to becoming one. Specialists will refine their knowledge through repeated evolutions, where they can hone their skills even more and sharpen their competitive edge in their market.

At the specialist level, Gary took charge of his father's liquor store, Shopper's Discount Liquors. He decided to forgo being a generalist like his father, who focused on selling all types of alcohol, and instead decided to specialize in the highest-grossing product: wine. He renamed his father's company to Wine Library and launched sales online, leveraging the power of e-commerce at a time when this was thought to be a risky maneuver. By hyper-focusing on the wine industry, he became a wine specialist. Gary knew that the wine market had a lot of potential, so he focused his expertise there. Strategically, this allowed him immense leverage that he didn't have when he was a generalist who was just the guy behind the counter at a random liquor store.

This period of specialization was crucial for Gary's success, and it taught him much-needed skills that laid the groundwork for his future ventures. Specializing allows you to marry your passion and expertise to gain momentum and grow your business.

Think about something you are deeply passionate about. How can you start to refine your skills like Gary did?

THE TAKEAWAY

Your focused expertise makes your advice more credible than generic tips. People seeking help in your area start recognizing you as someone who actually knows what they're talking about.

Level 3: The Authority

Mastery is a worthwhile pursuit, but it's a winding path. As Niels Bohr said, "An expert is a person who has made all the mistakes that can be made in a very narrow field." There's a reason that corporate executives at *Fortune* 500 companies usually have some gray hair. It takes time to learn the ropes and develop the skill sets that command respect in your profession. Similarly, it takes time to build up authority and influence online. Now, it can happen a lot quicker than it takes to climb the levels of the corporate ladder, but it still takes persistence and tenacity to get there.

After you reach the specialist level, you transition into true authority—but this isn't just about having expertise. Authority means you've authored original work, insights, or methods that have been validated by your peers and proven in the real world. Think peer-reviewed research, proprietary frameworks, or innovative approaches that others in your field recognize as legitimate.

But here's the challenge: Having authority and being known for it are two different things. Many brilliant authorities remain invisible because they haven't mastered the art of communication and promotion. This is where the path to thought leadership begins. To progress beyond basic authority, you must learn entirely new skills: creating content, building a platform, writing articles, getting featured on other experts' podcasts and shows, and yes, promoting yourself. It's no longer just about being right; it's about being seen and heard.

As you develop presence on camera (today's digital stage) and show up consistently, people start categorizing you in their minds as someone who doesn't just know things, but someone who thinks differently and can guide their thinking. The goal becomes showing up consistently and often so people recognize you as a thought leader in your space. You're literally learning to lead thoughts—to present original, unique perspectives that shape how people think.

Gary exemplifies this progression perfectly. He started *Wine Library TV*, a daily webcast on YouTube covering wine. This became his social-first show, allowing him to effectively star in his own show and operate like a Personal Media Company. He grew the business from $3 million a year to $60 million a year and began changing the landscape of his entire industry. He started influencing people to not only buy his wine online (a strange notion at the time) but to buy wine that they would like. His informative videos started influencing customer behavior at scale, and his influence grew thanks to his diligence in working with content, e-commerce, email marketing, and Google AdWords (now Google

Ads). By building a platform that established him as an authoritative thought leader, Gary changed the fundamental ways in which the wine industry operated. This helped him quickly rise through the ranks and become an authority figure for his entire industry.

THE TAKEAWAY

You have real expertise and proven results—the foundation is solid. But now comes the crucial shift: learning to promote yourself effectively. As you master content creation, platform building, and strategic positioning, you evolve from an unknown authority into a recognized thought leader. This is when you start achieving the "doctor effect"—in other words, your recommendations carry real weight, and people actually implement your advice. You're no longer just someone with credentials; you're someone whose thoughts shape how others think and act. This recognition as a thought leader positions you at the precipice of the next level, where true transformation begins.

Level 4: The Guru

Once you've established yourself as a thought leader whose advice people actually follow, the next level is scaling that influence into real transformation. The Guru's Journey intensifies here, as you must learn entirely new skills. This is where you transcend thought leadership and enter true guru territory. But remember, while this progression feels natural, the shift in responsibility and impact is significant. Gurus don't just lead, coach, or advise—they have the power to instill life-changing transformations that make a lasting impact and elevate everyone in their presence. The key difference? Gurus don't just have followers—they have believers. People who don't just consume their content but live by their teachings.

A thought leader will face important lessons on the path to guru status. The biggest shift between Level 3 and Level 4 comes down to where your priorities are aligned. If your heart is in the right place and you're focused on genuine service and transformation, the progression can happen naturally. If your heart is seeking the wrong things, like fame, fortune, and public accolades, then you risk becoming the kind of guru who exploits rather than empowers.

Moving up the Guru Ladder means your relationship with your audience changes. Early on, you're naturally focused on growth metrics and building your presence. But as you reach guru level, you realize that authentic influence comes from consistently delivering value, not from chasing the next viral moment.

While many gurus achieve celebrity-like status, their focus shifts at this level. Your influence becomes less about expanding your audience and more about deepening your impact. This is the difference between followers and believers. Influencers have followers who consume content. Gurus have believers who implement teachings and transform their lives. As a guru, you'll find that people from all over the globe genuinely value your insights and look to you for guidance on major life decisions.

Gurus are usually very likable people. They write books that become *New York Times* bestsellers, they appear on major TV shows, and they can sell out any venue they book. They have all the same characteristics as authorities do, but they've leveled up. They operate at a higher level. This combination of expertise, charisma, and platform creates significant leverage. At this level of influence, opportunities expand far beyond your core expertise. When you're an authority, your expertise is your commodity. As a guru, it is in fact *you* yourself who becomes the commodity— your personal transformation story, your unique perspective, and your ability to guide others become what people are really buying.

But this can be a slippery slope if you are still attached to your ego. Many gurus have fallen out of favor with their followers because they forgot who was serving whom. They get so attached to the praise and adoration of their audience that they start to create a cult of personality around their brand.

Level 4 is where the road narrows. The incline becomes steeper, and the path to success is a rickety old wooden-slat bridge that is missing a few boards. If you have faith, you can slowly walk across. If you are trapped in the fears of a scarcity mindset—clinging to external validation, ego boosts, and the need to be seen—you'll risk derailing your brand and losing your audience's trust.

When you reach Level 4, it means your life is dedicated to serving your followers. And if you commit to that high ideal of service, your life will change in indescribable ways. Doors you never even knew existed will swing open for you. And you will have the opportunity to develop rich, meaningful connections with your audience.

Let's go back to Gary's case study for a moment. Instead of being scared to open up about his passions, Gary saw that other people needed help mastering what he had already done. So he was brave enough to volunteer to help others. As he became more empowered to selflessly share his own personal story, fraught with failure, mishaps, and mistakes, he was able to gain traction and help more people. Sometimes, to help the greatest number of people, you have to be willing to take on notoriety. It can be scary, and imposter syndrome can flare up, but that's why there are levels to this process.

As Gary transitioned from authority to guru, something powerful happened. He stopped just teaching wine knowledge and started transforming how people saw entrepreneurship itself. Gary didn't just show people how to build businesses; he fundamentally shifted their relationship with work, proving that passion and profit could go hand in hand. His book *Crush It!* didn't just provide strategies—it gave people permission to turn their obsessions into empires. When Gary spoke about "crushing it," people didn't just get motivated for a day. They quit their jobs, started businesses, and completely reimagined what was possible for their careers. That's what separated Guru Gary from Thought Leader Gary: His followers didn't just learn from him, they *transformed* because of him. He didn't just influence thinking, he inspired life-changing action at massive scale. As a result, he became a highly sought-after celebrity voice in the business world, and whenever Guru Gary spoke, his followers listened.

THE TAKEAWAY

You're no longer just known for what you know, but for how you change people's lives. Your words don't just inform; they inspire action. People implement your frameworks, quit their jobs based on your advice, and reshape their worldview around your teachings. You're no longer selling knowledge; you're selling metamorphosis. The responsibility is immense, but so is the impact.

Level 5: The Guru's Guru

Finally, at the peak of influence comes the guru's guru: the ultimate visionary leader. The guru's guru no longer needs to promote themself, for they are known far and wide. Their Q score is off the charts (that's marketer's lingo for how recognizable someone is to the general public). In fact, they may rarely go out in public unnoticed by the time they reach this upper echelon. When they show up to an event, their influence draws a crowd. Everywhere they go, their followers are just a few steps behind them.

The guru's guru is someone who will be remembered in history. To put it in direct terms, a guru's guru transcends into popular culture. When you reach this status, you gain the magical key to open up perhaps the most powerful, influential, and lucrative business model that exists.

At this level, your Name, Image, and Likeness (NIL) becomes a formidable asset, intrinsically tied to your intellectual property—your unique frameworks, methods, and signature perspective. This combined force transforms your presence into the ultimate leverage point, attracting opportunities and partners with unparalleled ease. Instead of hustling to find opportunities and build your network, these things find you. Your well-defined NIL makes you a true magnet of opportunity. You have the Midas touch, where all you touch turns to gold. When you speak, people listen and take each of your words seriously because your identity commands trust and clarity. In a way, this is the top-of-the-mountain level, where you are elevated above the "rat race"—the business hustle that most humans have to endure their whole lives. Unusual things happen at this level. The universal formula of business flips on its head. You can shape reality, leveraging your established NIL to instantaneously connect with your audience at the push of a button in real time. This means you bypass all the gatekeepers.

By the time you reach Level 5, you realize that helping other people get from Level 4 to Level 5 will have the biggest impact on humanity. A *guru's guru* knows that if they help other gurus get to their level, it will exponentially help the world. This is the highest ideal of service. A prime example of this is Oprah Winfrey, who didn't just build her own empire but famously elevated figures like Dr. Phil and Dr. Oz, transforming them from experts into household names and significant thought leaders in their respective fields.

At the guru's guru level, ego doesn't disappear—it expands. And that expansion can be either a powerful asset or a dangerous liability. Some use it to serve a larger mission. Others use it to serve themselves. Level 5 gurus still possess strong egos—often huge ones. But the difference lies in what that ego is serving. Is it trying to be admired, feared, or worshipped? Or is it aligned with a legacy that transcends personal validation? If it's anchored in purpose, it fuels service, clarity, and leaves a positive mark on history and society. But if it's rooted in insecurity or performance, it can distort the mission entirely. The higher you rise, the more your ego becomes either an asset for serving others or a liability that isolates you.

At the apex of his success, Gary became the visionary thought leader behind VaynerX and subsidiary companies, which helped him create a true business empire. With millions of followers online, Gary can mentor and help other rising thought leaders break out in their industries. Gary is now a go-to resource and a top name in online entrepreneurship, making him synonymous with a "guru's guru." Gary can see ahead of the curve and anticipate market trends and underpriced attention. By using highly engaging storytelling to connect with his online audience, he is solidifying the prominence of his personal brand. As the name suggests, being a guru's guru means that Gary's most rewarding work isn't just achieving personal success, it is also mentoring others. He does this through his shows like The #AskGaryVee Show and DailyVee, which are designed to help inspire the next wave of entrepreneurs, influencers, and thought leaders in the business world and beyond. At Level 5, Gary unlocked the ultimate ability: turning his influence into a multimillion-dollar empire. And to think it all started with a lemonade stand!

When you reach this level, you have fully mastered behavioral influence. Your recommendations instantly alter markets, cultural trends, and even public opinion. At this apex, your word shapes reality on a massive scale, with millions immediately acting upon your insights. You embody the full power of what we discussed earlier, the "doctor effect," impacting society through direct behavioral change. Influence isn't just about attention. It's about action. Real thought leadership is when your audience consistently follows through on your recommendations. That's when influence translates from potential into the power of authentic transformation!

THE TAKEAWAY

You've unlocked the ultimate business superpower. Your name, image, and likeness generate wealth without your direct involvement. Opportunities come to you. Markets move when you speak. Your frameworks become industry standards that other experts teach. You're not just successful; you're the architect of success for an entire generation of leaders. This is the apex of influence, where legacy becomes your true currency.

It's important to understand that the Guru Ladder shows your external progression. It reflects how the world sees and responds to you. But moving up that ladder requires something deeper. Each level is powered by a phase of internal growth, which we call the Guru's Journey. These five levels are your roadmap in the new media game. Each one builds on the last, taking you from unknown expert to culture-shaping guru. The question isn't whether you can climb it. It's how far you're willing to evolve to get there.

Chapter 9

ATTENTION ECONOMICS

> Money flows where attention goes.
>
> —Steven Aitchison

If content creation is like a war, then the question is: How does one win the war? (Besides calling MrBeast and having him feature you as a contestant in one of those really entertaining challenge videos where you can win millions of dollars.)

To win the war for attention, you need to stand out in a battlefield full of other competitors all wanting the same thing, which is pretty intimidating, especially when you are competing with top-tier content creators like MrBeast and the endless new wave of breakout stars flooding the internet. But winning this war is not just about producing content—that's only part of the battle. Winning is more about strategic planning, continuous improvement, and relentless persistence to capture and hold your audience's attention. What stops most experts is that they are afraid to truly put themselves out there and commit to consistency. But before you can learn to do what my clients do (dominate their core social media interest spaces), you need to first understand the framework for how attention really works.

Social media basically hijacked all our brains, and none of us are getting free anytime soon. It captures our attention in dazzling displays of bite-size wisdom, entertainment, and education all wrapped into one tight short-form video. And whether we want to admit it or not, it really works. Social media generates more buzz about business, your child's soccer game, and world affairs than anything else on the planet. It also makes it extremely easy to get feedback and spread the word about your art, business, or your Pet Rock collection. I mean, where else can you network with thousands of people all in one place to look at your content? People are voting with their thumbs: If users like something, they will let you know by sharing it, commenting, or liking it.

Every time you post on social media, you capture a few seconds of someone's attention. It's a powerful tool, but the real question every content creator must ask is, "Who cares?" That's one of the challenges of our social media world. While an individual's attention is finite, the opportunities to connect with your specific audience are abundant. The goal isn't to compete for everyone's attention but to resonate deeply with the people who matter most. Many experts creating content fall into the trap of comparison, seeing flawless content and doubting themselves. But here's the truth: Behind those edits and perfectly timed videos, even the most successful content creators started where you are now, wrestling with the same doubts and uncertainties. The real secret isn't just getting attention—it's transforming it into trust and influence by building meaningful connections with your audience.

Some stuff on social media helps you; other stuff screws with your head. I won't belabor this point too much at this time. I'll discuss this at length later in this book so that you are ultimately using your influence ethically. However, I feel it is important to make this distinction before we start talking about attention in detail. Remember, I promised to guide you with some Jedi-level mind hacks, and if you are suffering under the zeitgeist of a limited thinking virus such as, "Wanting to get attention from other people is negative," you may be self-sabotaging your business pursuits on social media without even realizing it. So let's reframe this, shall we?

In 2024, people spent, on average, 143 minutes on social media per day.[7] That's over a month per year on social media! Researchers have estimated that the average person will spend more than five years of their lives on social media based on these projections. That may sound like a lot, but think about how much of your life is based on who and what you watch. Chances are, you don't call up all your friends and family every day to know if they are OK—you check their social media pages. You don't need to try every restaurant in your city; you can go online and check social media review pages first to narrow down your selection. So while five years may sound like a lot, social media is an exponentially powerful tool, which brings me to my larger point.

The attention you generate from your audience is the very fuel that helps you keep delivering your value to that audience. Put a different way, without attention, you can't make money to go on creating helpful content for your audience to consume. By that definition, attention is a good thing—a *very good* thing. In fact, attention is more like the new currency system in today's global social media economy.

The internet and television laid the foundation for what we now call the Attention Economy, where capturing audience focus became a valuable currency. Social media has accelerated this shift, ushering in the Creator Economy—a new era in which a person can directly build influence and turn their passions into businesses. In the past, success was controlled by gatekeepers: Record labels decided which musicians got promoted, publishers chose which books reached shelves, and television networks determined which shows aired. Today, it's not gatekeepers but audience attention that determines success. When someone follows you, watches your content, or engages with your posts, they're essentially "paying" you with their attention. That attention can then be transformed into business opportunities, influence, and revenue. Now anyone with a smartphone and internet connection can create content, reach an audience, and potentially make a living. This shift has democratized influence, making success less about gaining approval from traditional institutions and more about consistently delivering value that resonates with your audience. It's a fundamental change in how value is created and distributed in the digital world.

Look, attention is literally money now. Right this second, billions of people are scrolling on their phones. It has become the largest marketplace on Earth. The currency of attention is what people are really playing the new media game for. Most people assume that this marketplace is selling T-shirts, or gym products, or paid promotions for advertisers. They are wrong. Social media platforms are attention merchants, where you go to sell your attention in return for content. This is the new digital frontier, and if you want to succeed in our modern world, you need to learn how to leverage this digital currency.

Attention, unlike many commodities, cannot be stored or saved—once a moment of attention is spent, it's gone forever. *Poof!* Each person has only a limited amount of attention to use each day, making it one of the most precious and inherently scarce commodities available to creators. Scarcity is the cornerstone of economic value, which means attention is increasingly valuable precisely because it is limited.

With billions of posts uploaded daily, competition is intense. Each time you publish content, you're competing not just with direct rivals in your niche but with Netflix, TikTok trends, breaking news, and celebrity scandals. This intensifying competition raises the "cost" (in time, money, creativity, and effort) to capture and hold audience attention.

Every second spent on your content means your viewer actively chose you over infinite alternatives. This decision comes with an "opportunity cost"—the potential value or entertainment they're giving up elsewhere. The higher this cost, the higher your responsibility to deliver meaningful value, enhancing your own content's worth.

This shift has created what I call the "ACME" phenomenon: A Creator Making Everything. The old world of ACME (A Company Making Everything) was one in which large corporations controlled creation and distribution. Consider how General Electric went beyond just lightbulbs—they pioneered everything from home appliances to jet engines, even owning NBC for decades. In Japan, Mitsubishi wasn't just cars; at its peak, they made everything from beer to bank loans, televisions to cargo ships. Samsung transformed from a small grocery trading firm into a global giant that produces everything from smartphones to washing machines to insurance policies. But perhaps no company embodied this "make everything" approach more than Amazon, which evolved from an online bookstore into an empire spanning e-commerce, cloud computing, streaming entertainment, groceries, and even healthcare. Unlike these corporate giants of the past, the digital landscape now empowers people to build their own mini empires from home.

Once you establish an audience, you can monetize your passions in various ways, from selling online courses and launching products to writing books and securing brand deals. This transformation is happening across every field imaginable: cooking, art, gaming, fashion, and beyond. Popular content creators like Logan Paul and KSI turned their influence into the wildly successful Prime hydration brand; MrBeast launched Feastables, a fast-growing snack company; and Emma Chamberlain created Chamberlain Coffee, a lifestyle coffee brand that resonates with her devoted audience. The creative power is shifting from large soulless corporations to people like you. At the time of this writing, attention is the single most important asset you could have in your portfolio, and those who understand how to leverage this digital gold rush—through platforms, personal brands, and passionate audiences—are positioned to thrive.

Every time someone checks out your website or YouTube channel, you are getting their attention, even if it is just for a few seconds as they are quickly scrolling through their feeds while in line at the checkout counter. The best part is that your viewers can watch, read, or listen to your material without you having to be present. This may sound like it's not a big deal, but I invite you to think about how life was in the early 2000s. In case you weren't alive then, let me assure you, it was a very different world. All the activities you needed to run a successful business required immense amounts of time. Even today, a phone call or business meeting takes time—which is just another word for attention. But when you have evergreen content online, it stays there for night owls, foreign fans, and early birds alike to visit. This means that leveraging social media is a great trade in terms of your time invested. You trade some of your attention to create content, and you have the potential to have thousands of people watch your content while your attention is focused on other things. This leverage is what makes digital content so powerful in today's world.

In fact, this digital leverage has transformed how we approach every aspect of business and personal growth. Building your personal brand, networking at scale, and creating content aren't just online strategies—they're tools for accelerating your career, developing products, and building a real business. By establishing your presence in the digital space, you gain powerful leverage in the real world. It allows you to create opportunities, expand your reach, and position yourself as a leader in your field. The ability to connect with people globally and turn your expertise into something tangible is one of the most impactful ways to drive long-term success and growth.

Even if you're not active on social media or don't have many follow-ers, you can still start sharing your expertise effectively online. You don't need to be the smartest, the best looking, or a polished public speaker. What really matters is sharing bold ideas, offering fresh takes, or chal-lenging conventional thinking in your field.

Today's algorithms have shifted from the social graph (your network of friends and followers) to the interest graph (content people actively engage with). That means it's easier than ever to get discovered. Your content can reach people who are genuinely interested in your message, even if they've never heard of you before.

Many successful experts started by focusing on delivering real results through their content, like helping people achieve personal victories like improved health, financial stability, or renewed confidence. Once they proved they could get results, their brands grew organically into the kind of following we all aspire to build.

As we saw with Gary Vee, the more you commit to consistently delivering value, the faster you climb the Guru Ladder. But to truly maximize your business, you need to harness the exponential power of your audience's attention.

This isn't just about common sense. It's a game-changing shift in how businesses grow. In the digital age, attention is your most valuable resource. As my friend and marketing strategist Neil Patel says, "Success today is about achieving front-row visibility on your digital channels, oftentimes without even being clicked. It's like a Formula One car cov-ered in logos. Most people can't name the sponsors, but they've seen those logos hundreds of times. That's brand memory. You're not just playing for traffic anymore; you're playing for recognition."

When you free up your time and focus your energy on high-impact content, you create room for deeper innovation and business growth. That's how you scale your influence and unlock your full creative potential.

THE REAL ADHD

To help illustrate my point, I want to give you a powerful acronym. We are currently living in the time of ADHD. No, not the ADHD you've probably heard of that plagues students and parents across the United States. (I'm not talking about the Kendrick Lamar song, either.) Despite the fact that all of us are super distracted by our phones nowadays, what I'm talking about is the concept of how attention is monetized.

Or, to use an acronym—ADHD: *Attention drives high dollars.*

MrBeast is a perfect example of how attention can be transformed into unparalleled opportunities. With over 395 million subscribers across his YouTube channels as of May 2025—more than the population of the United States—he's built a business empire by consistently delivering high-impact, engaging content. His success extends far beyond YouTube. From launching Feastables, a thriving snack company, to reportedly turning down a $1 billion offer for his brand, MrBeast has demonstrated the immense value of strategically managing attention. In 2024, he secured a $100 million deal with Amazon MGM Studios to produce *Beast Games*, a groundbreaking reality competition series. This show, with a $5 million cash prize and a custom-built "Beast City," exemplifies how content creators can leverage their audience's attention to command budgets and influence that rival traditional media giants. His story illustrates the power of playing the long game, consistently creating content, and turning attention into high-dollar opportunities.

THE IMPORTANCE OF PARASOCIAL RELATIONSHIPS

The big thing that I feel is missing in most conversations around social media dynamics is the psychological concept known as parasocial relationships. A parasocial relationship is a one-sided relationship a person has with a media figure they don't know. This is the backdrop for how social media impacts people and drives their behavior, often in competitive ways. Parasocial relationships are formed when someone "knows" you online but has never met you in person.

Despite the fact that you've never met, people start to form these relationships with your content, your image, and, yes, even your thought leadership—but not you. What that means for content creators in the digital age is that your followers feel like they know you, even though they don't. This can help you leverage your expertise to get them anticipating your future content. But remember, if they lose interest, you lose their attention. This is why you really want to do your best to foster real, authentic relationships with your followers. But as any thought leader knows, this is a skill that takes time to master.

Attention is the name of the game when it comes to ascending the Five Levels of the Guru Ladder. You could say that the more attention you generate, the faster you climb up each of the levels. But the question you are probably asking is: Once you generate all this attention, how do you turn that attention into real, sustainable business growth? Stay tuned—that is a question we will tackle in the next chapter. For now, the important thing to remember is that as you ascend, you will constantly have to refresh and reinvent your content to keep evolving. Economics has this thing called a saturation point—basically, there's only so much of anything people can consume before they've had enough. As an avid content consumer, you quickly realize there's always a new "flavor of the week"—content creators who skyrocket to popularity only to gradually fade away. While some manage to maintain relevance or brilliantly reinvent themselves, others inevitably succumb to the relentless churn of the creator economy and hit their audience's saturation point. Take the "Costco Guys," who gained fame for their enthusiastic takes on the chicken bake and "double chunk chocolate cookie" (and yes, I hope you heard Big Justice and A.J.'s voices in your head when I said that). They demonstrated remarkable agility by reinventing themselves through col-laborations and smart career moves.

Every piece of content you create should be a deliberate step in your journey from generalist to specialist, from specialist to authority, and beyond. Even if you don't hit a home run every time, being intentional with how you stairstep your content will draw more attention over time. This approach not only builds trust but may even spark word-of-mouth buzz from people in real life. Word of mouth remains one of the most powerful ways to grow your audience and attract new clients. At the same time, remember that every content creator you watch is navigating the same intersection of art and commercialization. Monetizing through sponsored posts, partnerships, or product promotions is a necessity for sustaining their livelihood. But there's a delicate balance—when creators overly focus on selling out to money grabs, they risk losing the very trust and connection that set them apart. The key is to prioritize authentic, valuable content that fosters long-term trust, making your audience seek your perspective and stay loyal, even as you grow.

The number one reason most people fail to capitalize on the abun-dance of attention on social media is a lack of consistency and strategic positioning. While it's easy to post sporadically when inspiration strikes, real growth comes from adopting a media company mindset—thinking of your presence as your own show with ongoing programming. This means blending your core expertise with your unique interests, revealing the multifaceted nature of who you are while developing a distinct per-spective that sets you apart as a leader in your niche. Most people treat social media informally, like chatting with friends, without crafting a clear point of view or reliable value delivery. Without intentional posi-tioning, you blend into the crowd and risk losing the war for attention. To stand out, you must own your niche, be known for something spe-cific, and train both the algorithm and your audience to pay attention every time you post.

This brings us to a fundamental question in the game of attention: How do you convert attention into tangible business outcomes—into real dollars? While surface metrics like likes and shares provide some feedback, they don't reflect the true value of attention or how it translates into career and business growth. It can feel disheartening to pour time and money into creating content without seeing clear, immediate returns—sometimes for months or even years. The experts preaching content creation at the highest levels tell us to play the long game, to build a personal brand, but it often feels like navigating in the dark. So how do you stay focused and keep going when the path isn't always clear? The answer lies in understanding the true mechanics of attention economics. We've explored how attention drives high dollars (ADHD), how the Creator Economy has democratized influence, and how parasocial relationships and satiation points affect the growth and positioning of your brand. But to truly capitalize on these dynamics, you need a systematic way to measure and optimize your efforts—a framework that connects attention to actual business outcomes. I've developed exactly that. It's called . . .

Chapter 10

RETURN ON ATTENTION CREATED

Not everything that can be counted counts.

—William Bruce Cameron[8]

The Weeknd performed at the 2021 Super Bowl halftime show for free. Zero dollars. Meanwhile, brands paid $5.5 million for a 30-second ad slot. Why would a global superstar work for nothing? Because he understood something most people miss about attention.

At first glance, the Super Bowl seems like just a football game, but in reality, it is a masterclass in Return on Attention Created (ROAC). Don't believe me? Consider this: Year after year, the Super Bowl attracts hundreds of millions of viewers, demands some of the highest advertising rates in history, and dominates social media engagement like no other event. But the real takeaway isn't just about capturing attention, it's about what happens next. Because attention, on its own, isn't inherently valuable. The real power lies in how you leverage, sustain, and monetize it.

Still not convinced? Let's take a closer look at what makes the Super Bowl a case study in attention monetization.

THE POWER OF ATTENTION AS A CURRENCY

Did you know that Super Bowl halftime performers don't get paid a single dollar for their performance? It's true. Instead of a big paycheck, they receive something far more valuable: attention.

Even though the NFL used to pay its halftime performers millions of dollars, today, top artists like Rihanna, The Weeknd, and Beyoncé perform for free during halftime. Why? Because the attention they receive during the Super Bowl translates into explosive growth for their personal brands.

Take The Weeknd's 2021 Super Bowl Halftime performance as an example. After the show, his Spotify streams surged by nearly 220% in the United States.

These artists understand that attention drives high dollars—far more than any direct paycheck could offer. Brands know this, too, which is why a 30-second Super Bowl ad in 2025 cost $8 million—proof that attention has become one of the most sought-after commodities in today's economy.[9]

ATTENTION MERCHANTS

The Super Bowl is just a rare example of a high-visibility moment of mass attention. In today's digital world, attention is bought, sold, and traded every second. And that brings us to the real marketplace of attention: social media.

Every day, digital platforms function as true attention marketplaces where brands, creators, and businesses battle for visibility. Platforms like Facebook, Instagram, TikTok, YouTube, and Google are what I like to call "attention merchants." Their entire business model revolves around one thing: selling your attention to the highest bidder. Every time you scroll, like, or engage, your attention is being auctioned off in real time to brands that want to pay big money for it. *Attention drives high dollars.*

This system has given rise to the Creator Economy, a rapidly growing industry already valued at over $250 billion in 2023, with Goldman Sachs projecting it to nearly double by 2027.[10] In this new landscape, individuals can monetize their personal brands and content just like companies do. But in a world where attention is the most valuable currency, the real challenge isn't just getting seen—it's turning that attention into actual business value.

In 2025 and beyond, the smartest creators aren't asking, "How many people watched my video?" They're asking, "What happened because people watched it?" That's the difference between vanity and value.

STOP COUNTING LIKES, START COUNTING IMPACT

When I first started working with personal brands back in 2012, my focus was on helping experts turn their knowledge into thriving digital businesses. I partnered with a sales trainer who went on to sell hundreds of thousands of dollars in coaching programs, an author who went on to become a three-time *New York Times* bestseller, and a TV star who turned their online presence into a personal media empire generating millions in revenue.

I watched the digital world evolve rapidly. Traditional media was fading, and social media was taking over as the new stage for influence and authority. Podcasts, YouTube, and social video weren't just trends; they were the future of content consumption. But as I worked with these brands, I encountered a frustrating problem: While their digital presence was growing, it was nearly impossible to quantify the actual business impact of the attention they were generating.

Take this for example: A client would land a multimillion-dollar deal just because someone "saw them on Instagram." Or a YouTube video would unexpectedly drive a surge of high ticket sales. The results were undeniable, but how could we measure or prove where they actually came from? The impact was real, but tracking it felt like trying to catch smoke.

I started to realize something: We were measuring success all wrong.

Most marketers were obsessed with vanity metrics: views, likes, shares. And I get it. These numbers feel like progress. They tell you that people are paying attention. But here's the problem: Attention alone doesn't build businesses, value does.

That's when I met my business advisor, Roy Cammarano. A seasoned executive and author, Roy had built multiple Inc. 500 companies and understood how businesses create long-term value. As we worked together, he helped me see that the real question wasn't just how much attention you get, but what that attention turns into. Together, we developed a simple way to measure the value your content actually creates.

We called it ROAC: return on attention created.

THE ROAC MINDSET: BEYOND THE NUMBERS

Think about it. A million views may look impressive, but what do they actually mean if they don't lead to anything? Likes don't pay the bills. Engagement doesn't guarantee impact. What really matters isn't just getting people to notice you, it's how that attention translates into action, relationships, and opportunities.

This is exactly where most brands and creators go wrong. They focus on maximizing attention, but they don't think about what to do with it. That's why ROAC shifts the focus away from raw visibility and toward what actually counts: the real-world value your content creates and, more importantly, how you can make that value come back to you.

The truth is, not all attention creates the same value. Some content gets you noticed. Other content gets you hired. And the best content? It changes lives—including your own. Here's what I mean. When you start paying attention to impact instead of metrics, you'll notice three things happening:

Sometimes the impact is immediate: Your content drives sales, sign-ups, or leads. Someone reads your advice and takes action right away.

Sometimes it builds your reputation: Your expertise gets recognized by other experts. A CEO shares your post, then invites you to speak at their conference. A psychologist validates your advice publicly.

And sometimes it transforms lives: Your message helps someone set boundaries at work, or makes them feel understood for the first time.

Let me show you what this looks like in practice. A video about burnout racks up 100,000 views. On the surface, those are good numbers. But the real win? A DM from someone who says, "This made me finally book therapy and I haven't missed a session since." A podcast clip gets 75 shares. Surface level? Decent engagement. But one of those shares comes from a CEO who ends up inviting you to keynote their company retreat for $10,000. A post gets 500 likes. Not bad. But buried in the comments? A former client tags a friend and says, "Working with this person changed my business." That single comment brings in three new leads.

See the difference? The numbers tell you people were watching. The stories tell you your content moved something. That's what separates creators who chase attention from those who convert it.

WHEN ATTENTION BECOMES AUTHORITY

Here's something most content creators miss: The real value of a post isn't just how many people watch. It's who is watching. When the right person sees your content, everything can change. If a respected expert shares your post or a verified professional publicly backs your advice, their credibility doesn't just stay with them. It carries over to you. That kind of trust transfer is how attention turns into real value.

Social media is more than a numbers game. It's a web of relationships. When high-authority figures engage with your content, their interaction amplifies your message and boosts your perceived authority in ways that raw views or likes never could. This kind of attention is worth more than any vanity metric.

A perfect example of this in action involves my client Warren Phillips, better known as "Non-Toxic Dad," a health and wellness expert who has built a highly engaged community around clean living and non-toxic products through his social media channels. We created a video where Warren discussed the hidden dangers of air fresheners. This single piece of content generated over 10 million views, thousands of shares, and more than 10,000 engagements on Instagram Reels alone. Quantitatively, the impact was clear.

But qualitatively, something even more valuable happened. People started resharing Warren's video with their own commentary. One standout came from a doctor who filmed himself in medical scrubs endorsing Warren's message. This doctor's video gained over two million views within the first 24 hours alone, significantly amplifying Warren's credibility and authority.

The doctor's endorsement did more than just increase view counts; it elevated Warren's brand equity by associating him and his advice with medical expertise and authoritative validation. This type of high-quality interaction is incredibly valuable, as it shapes audience perception, enhances credibility, and positions Warren as a trusted guru in his niche. That's ROAC in action.

THREE SIMPLE WAYS TO MAKE YOUR CONTENT COUNT

Step 1: Create Content Worth Remembering

Getting attention is easy. Keeping it and turning your content into something meaningful that resonates with your audience over time? That's the real challenge. To maximize ROAC, your content has to do more than just attract views—it needs to inspire action, spark conversations, and build relationships.

How to do it:

- **Know what keeps your audience up at night.** What problems are they trying to solve? What dreams are they chasing? Your best content lives at the intersection of their struggles and your solutions.
- **Give every piece of content a job.** Before you hit publish, ask: What do I want someone to do after watching this? Feel inspired? Take action? Share with a friend? If you don't know, neither will they.
- **Meet people where they are.** Short-form videos? Long-form videos? Podcasts? Choose based on where your audience is most active and how they prefer to engage.
- **Make sure the right people see it.** Your content isn't valuable if no one sees it. Use social media, email marketing, SEO, and partnerships to ensure your content reaches the right people at the right time.

Step 2: Pay Attention to What Really Matters

Engagement metrics don't tell the full story. A video can have thousands of views and likes but still fail to create real impact, and the same thing is true the other way around. Instead of chasing numbers, start tracking the actual effect your content has on people's lives and decisions.

How to do it:

- **Listen beyond the metrics.** Comments, direct messages, and emails often tell a richer story than likes and shares. Look for messages that express how your content really helped someone. Screenshot those messages—they're your real success metrics.
- **Watch for action, not just reaction.** Are people actually implementing your advice? Are they tagging you in their own success stories? That's the real sign your content is making a difference.
- **Keep it simple.** Did your content lead to immediate results? Build your reputation over time? Or transform how someone thinks? All three count, but knowing which is which helps you create more of what works.

Step 3: Do More of What's Working

If you're not learning from your content's performance, you're leaving growth on the table. Once you understand the real impact of your content, the next step is to optimize and scale your strategy in a way that compounds over time.

How to do it:

- **Spot the patterns.** Which posts get people taking action? Which ones get shared by other experts? Which ones generate real business results? Double down on those.
- **Turn success into more success.** Use stories of impact in marketing, sales, and internal communications to demonstrate the real-world value of your expertise.
- **Find your people.** Connect with other creators and thought leaders who share your values. Their audiences might need exactly what you're offering.

Let me show you how this plays out in the real world.

ROAC IN ACTION: THE CASE STUDIES

The Mariah Effect: Turning a One-Time Investment into a Lifetime of Returns

Every year, like clockwork, the holiday season arrives, and Mariah Carey's "All I Want for Christmas Is You" takes over.

It's in stores, on playlists, in commercials—it's everywhere. But what makes this song so special? Why, over three decades after its release, is it still a cultural and commercial phenomenon?

The answer is simple: ROAC.

Instead of fading into nostalgia like most holiday songs, Mariah's "All I Want for Christmas Is You," written in 1994, remains a cultural reset button every November. Why? Because it taps into an emotionally charged tradition—the universal excitement of the holiday season. And that emotional connection is the secret to transformational ROAC.

Mariah's ability to capture attention once and continually reap the benefits year after year—the track has generated over $60 million in royalties and continues to dominate the charts every holiday season—is the ultimate goal of content creators. Her song is an asset, one that requires no additional effort but continues to deliver returns in the form of:

- Ongoing royalties from streaming and radio play
- New collaborations (like her duet with Justin Bieber, exposing her music to younger audiences)
- Brand deals and licensing opportunities that keep her culturally relevant

This is the power of intentional content creation: You invest effort into something once, and it pays off forever. Many artists have tried to replicate Mariah's success by releasing Christmas songs, but few have managed to reach the same level of cultural permanence. Why? Because

ROAC isn't just about capturing attention, it's about creating something people want to return to, over and over again.

A few hours of creativity turned into a lifetime of revenue, influence, and brand longevity. Let that sink in.

Nikki Haskell, the Grandfluencer: Reinventing Relevance Through ROAC

This approach can work at any age, even when conventional wisdom says you're "too old" for social media.

Let me tell you about Nikki Haskell.

Nikki was a trailblazer in the '80s, hosting her own celebrity talk show and rubbing shoulders with the biggest names in Hollywood. But by the time she hit *her* eighties, she had faded from the public eye. Social media had reshaped the entertainment industry, and younger generations had no idea who she was. To make matters more challenging, Nikki had received negative press in recent years, making it even harder to reclaim her relevance.

So how does someone go from *forgotten* to *thriving* in a space dominated by digital natives?

By focusing on what actually mattered: real impact over vanity metrics.

Nikki wasn't a natural fit for TikTok; in fact she was far from it. She was unfamiliar with the platform, the culture, and the trends. But we experimented. We tested different types of content to see what resonated. And then, we found it: a social-first show about an 80-year-old woman giving no-nonsense, unfiltered life advice to twentysomethings.

That was the magic formula.

Her videos took off. Almost overnight, she became a viral sensation. But more than just numbers, Nikki's success demonstrated the power of ROAC. She wasn't just getting views; she was reshaping perceptions.

By leaning into humor, authenticity, and her decades of wisdom, Nikki transformed into what the internet now calls a "grandfluencer"—a new category of content creators who bridge generational gaps and bring fresh perspectives to younger audiences.

The results?

- Millions of monthly views across TikTok and Instagram
- Regular engagement from celebrities and influencers, including Paris Hilton
- Brand deals with major companies, new business opportunities, media appearances, and collabs

This wasn't just attention—it was attention that built authority, credibility, and influence.

But what really validated our approach wasn't found in any analytics dashboard. It was when Nikki started sharing stories about her daily life. People approaching her at restaurants, stopping her on the streets, asking for photos at events. Strangers telling her how much her advice had changed their lives. These moments showed us that her content wasn't just getting views, it was creating genuine connections and real impact.

What Nikki's story proves is that ROAC isn't just about being famous—it's about positioning, reinvention, and leveraging attention into real-world opportunities. She turned fleeting digital engagement into sustained influence, proving that it's never too late to build a brand that matters.

This is the power of measuring what matters instead of what's easy to track. When you stop counting likes and start counting lives changed, opportunities created, and relationships built, you transform from someone who just gets attention into someone who commands respect.

Here's the beautiful paradox: Once you shift your focus to real impact, those vanity metrics suddenly aren't so vain anymore. A thousand views means something when you know your content actually helps people. A hundred shares carries weight when you're tracking how your message spreads. The numbers gain context and meaning because you're measuring them against what actually matters—transformation, not just transaction. That's how attention becomes authority, and authority becomes everything else you want to build.

Chapter 11
THE HIDDEN LANGUAGE OF VIRALITY

The best way to predict the future is to create it.

—Peter Drucker

During the tragic loss of Kobe Bryant, something unexpected happened that changed how I understood viral content. A helicopter crash sent shockwaves across Los Angeles that were felt all around the world. Kobe Bryant had just passed away, and 2020 was shaping up to be a year of unprecedented change. In the few short months between his death in January and the COVID-19 lockdowns in March, a new online social media platform called TikTok was rapidly gaining momentum. While many saw it as just another fleeting social media fad, I knew that there was an opportunity to seize and capture a new share of the market on a fresh platform. As a digital native (a term I'll explain more later), TikTok reminded me of one of its earlier predecessors called Vine, so I decided to test it out.

I saw someone mention an eerie numerical connection between Kobe's jersey numbers and the years of Kobe and his daughter Gigi's lives on an Instagram graphic. It caught my attention. I decided to make a short video about it, mixing a bit of curiosity, suspense, and emotion. (Pay close attention to the three-act structure that I employed. Take a mental screenshot of it, because I will come back to it later.)

1. **Opening Hook:** A shot of me thinking, with text on the screen:
   Kobe Bryant 1978–2020
   Gigi Bryant 2006–2020
2. **The Buildup:** A scene of me pretending to add numbers on my fingers while the text shows:
   1978 + 2020 + 2006 + 2020 = 8024
3. **The Payoff:** My shocked reaction as the numbers 8 and 24 (Kobe's jersey numbers) appear, paired with dramatic music and a caption:
   "Try the math yourself. Legends never die."

I hit "publish." Then I made myself a sandwich and forgot all about it. I didn't think anything of it until my brother called me to tell me the news: "Dude, you went viral!"

Within 24 hours, the video had over one million views. Comments flooded in. My follower count skyrocketed. And just like that, I had gone viral. One million pairs of eyeballs had seen my post. One million people had paid attention to this small tidbit of information about the life of NBA legend Kobe Bryant.

But here's what most people won't tell you about virality: Not all attention is equally valuable. Yes, the video blew up, but it attracted an audience that had nothing to do with my actual brand. These weren't people interested in marketing, content strategy, or thought leadership. They were just captivated by a random numerical coincidence tied to a trending topic. The views were high, but the impact wasn't there. Even worse, I had no way to replicate my success.

Going viral isn't just luck—it's a strategic move in the attention game. Just like chess has opening moves that set you up for success, viral content follows patterns you can learn and repeat. That day in 2020, I learned a crucial lesson: Virality alone means nothing if it doesn't serve your brand, your message, or your long-term vision. Getting millions of views is easy; turning those views into real influence is the hard part. The goal isn't just to go viral—it's to go viral in a way that builds lasting authority.

This led me on a journey to study and try to reverse-engineer the phenomenon of going viral. Most people assume going viral is just dumb luck, but as I quickly found out, there's actually a lot of science behind it. And once you understand the hidden structure, you can engineer viral content intentionally instead of hoping for lightning to strike twice.

The real secret is that there is a hidden language of virality operating in the background that goes beyond just the algorithm, unbeknownst to the masses of social media users. Since you are reading this book, you are no longer a passive viewer. You are now a student of how content works. You must dedicate yourself to learning how and why these principles work so that you can replicate successful social media strategies that other gurus employ for yourself. To understand how to pull off this feat, we can look to cutting-edge neuroscience.

According to a published study conducted in 1973 by Daniel Kahneman, attention is a finite cognitive resource, and in a world flooded with content, getting noticed is harder than ever. When content goes viral, it breaks through the noise and seizes a disproportionate share of attention, giving the creator a rare opportunity to establish dominance in their niche.

Consistent virality means winning the "war for attention" and standing out in an oversaturated market. Viral content is successful not just because it gets seen, but because it secures a temporary monopoly on audience focus, which can be leveraged to build long-term brand equity.

This is why I never place too much importance on clients who just want to "go viral." I think of random virality like a sugar rush—a quick high followed by a crash. What you really want is sustainable energy that comes from consistently showing up and delivering value. Because attention is social currency, and you have to choose carefully how you spend it.

THE HIDDEN LANGUAGE OF VIRAL CONTENT

To get a better understanding of what I mean, let's compare virality with a concept that a lot of people enjoy: drinking wine. While wine may be seen as a leisurely pastime with friends—something casual and random you do to feel better—many people take it very seriously. There is an entire industry with schools, courses, vineyard tours, and businesses that cater to helping people dive deeper into their passion for the fruity drink of the gods.

Most people judge a video the same way they judge a glass of wine. They either like it, or they shrug their shoulders and say it was OK. But a sommelier, a true student of wine, can describe the exact notes that create a wine's experience. If you want to master content as an expert and eventually create viral videos of your own, you also need to be able to identify the elements that make a good video go viral.

A sommelier doesn't just say a wine tastes good and stop there. They break it down into rich descriptive classifications—there's a hidden language of ranking that takes place behind the scenes. They have trained their palate to detect the subtle nuances such as "oaky notes," "bright acidity," or a "velvety finish"—all of which interact with your senses to create a specific experience.

Content works the same way. When a video holds your attention, there's a reason. Maybe it's a "curiosity hook" that pulls you in, a "pattern interruption" that surprises you, or an "emotional arc" that keeps you invested. These elements aren't random. They are strategic. They can be identified, studied, and used intentionally to create videos that consistently resonate with audiences. The brilliance behind learning this secret language is that once you know it, you can't unsee it. Then, you can use these techniques to replicate your success and diagnose where you missed the mark in future attempts.

THE ELEMENTS OF IRRESISTIBLE CONTENT

Just as wine experts can break down what makes a wine good, you can break down what makes content work. Here's what you need to know to begin diagnosing how to improve the virality of your content.

1. Curiosity Hooks: The First Sip

A great wine intrigues you from the first sip. A strong hook triggers curiosity within seconds. It taps into the brain's "curiosity gap"—the need to fill in missing information.

Think about viral videos that start with, "You won't believe what happened when . . ." That's not accidental. It's a psychological trigger intentionally employed to keep you watching.

In my personal example at the beginning of this chapter, I knew that posting about Kobe Bryant was timely because people were eating up any content they saw about him. I made sure to include a strong, compelling hook to get them to fight the urge to keep scrolling. You can do this by calling their mind back to something nostalgic, teaching them how to overcome a problem they are currently facing, or explaining something they are curious about.

This isn't just theory. It's something neuroscientists call the "Zeigarnik effect," which was discovered in 1927. According to Bluma

Zeigarnik, unfinished or suspenseful stories create a psychological pull, keeping audiences hooked. You can leverage this for yourself by leveraging cliffhangers, teasers, or open-ended narratives, keeping audiences invested and encouraging binge consumption.

Just as tannins in wine physically interact with proteins in your mouth, video elements trigger actual neurological responses. A pattern interruption can cause a micro-dopamine hit. A well-placed hook can create an unresolved tension that compels someone to keep watching. And just as winemakers use their expertise to craft unforgettable wines, great content creators don't rely on chance—they use these principles deliberately to shape audience perception and drive engagement. This is the first example for a reason. *The hook is the most important part of the video.* If you don't catch their attention right away, they'll keep scrolling.

2. Emotional Arcs: The Full-Bodied Experience

A well-structured video is like a well-balanced wine, evolving with every moment. In creative writing classes, they teach you how to structure story arcs that keep the reader interested and, more importantly, *emotionally invested.* Just as a great wine transitions from one flavor note to another as it swishes around your mouth, a compelling video guides the viewer through an emotional journey. It starts with surprise, leading to laughter, and ends with reflection.

When emotions shift throughout a video, audiences stay engaged. They don't just watch; they feel that transformation of sensory experiences in real time. Ideally, they end up somewhere they weren't expecting to go, like how I showed people that there was something more than meets the eye about the numerology involved in Kobe's death. It's like going on a roller coaster with a stranger. At the beginning, you hardly know each other, but after going on an exhilarating ride together, you have shared a bond that has the potential to spark a conversation or shared laugh that can lead to the beginning of a friendship.

3. Pattern Interruptions: The Unexpected Spice

Ever tasted a wine with an unexpected burst of spice? It jolts your senses, wakes up your taste buds, and makes you pay attention to it. In video content, "pattern interruptions" do the exact same thing.

These are sudden shifts: an unexpected visual, a change in tone, or an abrupt pause that snaps the brain out of autopilot and forces engagement. This is why smart creators weave in unexpected moments to reset viewer attention and extend watch time. It keeps people engaged because it provides their brain with something novel to focus on. As humans we are hardwired to pay attention to things we haven't encountered before. It's the same drive that makes us want to travel, or check out a new movie, or listen to a new band. Variety helps the brain become more neuroplastic, which creates new neural pathways and strengthens our associations. When this occurs, it is the brain's version of "lifting weights," helping us learn and retain new information.

HOW CONTENT CREATORS CAN USE THIS

Great content isn't just about aesthetics. It's not about how you look or how much you spend on a videographer. The more important reality is about understanding the invisible forces that hold your audience's attention. Just like a sommelier can predict which wines will age well, a skilled content creator can predict which content elements will perform well with specific audiences.

By learning this hidden language, you stop guessing and start creating with intention. That's the difference between hoping for virality and engineering content that resonates. Curiosity fuels clicks. Strong hooks create a need for closure and keep your audience watching until the very end. Emotional shifts sustain your audience's attention. The best videos take viewers on a journey. Pattern interruptions reignite engagement. Unexpected moments keep people watching. This is how the human brain is wired: We all want to solve the riddle of plot and close these open loops. It's just human nature. So what can you do to master the study of viral content to replicate it in your brand?

It's really simple. The next time you find yourself glued to a video, try to break it down. Save it to your saved folder and try to identify what the strengths of the video were. What was the reason you kept watching? Was it the hook, the pacing, the tension? Next, try to replicate the strengths of the video in your next content piece. When you learn the language of content, you start seeing patterns everywhere. And once you understand how the elements work, you can start using them intentionally. That's when content creation stops being a guessing game and becomes a true craft.

THE HIDDEN LANGUAGE ONE-PAGER
(THAT I WANT YOU TO STEAL)

Remember in high school when you would have vocabulary tests in English class? At first, they may have seemed really difficult, but when you start learning and memorizing nifty tricks like studying Latin roots (the basis for our language), it demystifies the meanings. Instead of memorizing one word at a time, you can intuitively grasp the concepts behind dozens of words just by remembering a few prefixes and suffixes. This may seem like a Jedi mind trick, but it's a life hack that you can apply to creating viral content too. All you have to do is learn the hidden language that governs it.

To help you learn this secret language, I'm going to let you steal a page out of the social media playbook that I share with my clients. This is something that I go into in way more depth in online training programs, but here's the core structure you can start using right away.

This framework is specifically designed for organic social media content, focusing on virality, engagement, and audience building—*not* ads or conversions. I suggest that you write this down on a piece of paper, type it out on your phone, and save it as your screensaver background, or print it out and tape it to your desktop so that you can always have access to it wherever you make your content.

1. The Hook: Capturing Attention

The goal is to stop the scroll and immediately intrigue the viewer.

1. **Curiosity Hook:** Creates an information gap that the brain wants to close. (Example: "This one mistake cost me everything . . .")
2. **Shock Factor:** Uses extreme or unexpected statements to grab attention. (Example: "Your phone is dirtier than a toilet seat.")
3. **Pattern Interruption:** Breaks the expected flow with sudden visual or narrative shifts. (Example: Quick zooms, abrupt cuts, loud sound effects.)
4. **Misdirection:** Leads the audience one way, then delivers an unexpected twist. (Example: "I thought I was getting fired, but instead . . .")
5. **Urgency & Scarcity:** Adds a reason to watch now rather than later. (Example: "This video won't be up for long.")

2. The Hold: Retaining Attention

Once a viewer starts watching, these techniques ensure they stay engaged and watch longer.

1. **Story Loop:** Opens an unresolved question or scenario that forces viewers to stick around for the answer. (Example: "Before I tell you what happened, here's some context . . .")

2. **Emotional Arc:** Guides viewers through a structured emotional journey, keeping them invested. (Example: Starting with excitement, moving to conflict, and ending with resolution.)

3. **Contrast Framing:** Uses strong opposites to keep viewers intrigued. (Example: "$10 meal vs. $1,000 meal—what's the difference?")

4. **Callbacks:** References something earlier in the video to create a payoff moment. (Example: "Remember when I said this would be important? Here's why.")

5. **Surprise & Delight:** Adds an unexpected reward to keep viewers engaged. (Example: "Stay until the end for a secret tip.")

3. The Interaction: Encouraging Engagement

These elements maximize likes, comments, and shares, which increase organic reach.

1. **Controversial Positioning:** Expresses a strong opinion that sparks debate. (Example: "AI will replace 90% of jobs—prove me wrong.")

2. **Hot Takes & Contrarian Views:** Challenges mainstream beliefs to attract discussion. (Example: "Most morning routines are a waste of time.")

3. **Tribal Identity Content:** Reinforces a group's beliefs, leading to strong support or backlash. (Example: "Real entrepreneurs don't have a backup plan.")

4. **Audience Participation Prompts:** Directly invites viewers to comment or engage. (Example: "What's your worst travel experience? Drop it below.")

5. **Opinion Polling:** Directs the audience to take a stance and engage. (Example: "Which side are you on: A or B? Comment below.")

4. The Shareability Factor: Increasing Reach

These elements make content more likely to be shared, expanding its organic distribution.

1. **Relatability:** Content that reflects a common experience or feeling. (Example: "We've all been here . . .")
2. **Hyperbole & Exaggeration:** Amplifies an idea to make it more engaging. (Example: "This is the hardest challenge on the internet.")
3. **Nostalgia Triggers:** Leverages past experiences to create an emotional reaction. (Example: "Only '90s kids will remember this.")
4. **Tag-a-Friend CTA:** Encourages sharing by making viewers think of someone else. (Example: "Tag a friend who needs to see this.")
5. **Unexpected Twists:** Makes content more surprising and memorable. (Example: "At first, I thought this was a scam, but then . . .")

5. The Memorability Factor: Leaving a Lasting Impression

These techniques make content stick in the audience's mind and encourage repeat viewership.

1. **Signature Catchphrase or Style:** A repeated phrase or unique way of presenting content. (Example: Social media food vlogger Keith Lee's "I got it, let's try it, and rate it one through 10.")

2. **Edutainment:** Combines education with entertainment to make learning fun. (Example: Bill Nye the Science Guy explaining a complex topic in a humorous way.)

3. **Metaphors & Analogies:** Simplifies complex ideas using familiar comparisons. (Example: "Social media is like dating—you need to build trust first.")

4. **Looping Endings:** A seamless ending that encourages rewatching. (Example: Video ends exactly where it started, making viewers want to replay it.)

5. **Emotional Closure:** Ends with a strong takeaway that sticks. (Example: "If you take one thing from this video, remember this . . .")

THE "MONKEY SEE, MONKEY DO" PRINCIPLE

Humans are hardwired to imitate what works. We mirror success. It's how we learn language, culture, and behavior. And it's how we learn to create content too. When we see someone win online, our brains instinctively want to reverse-engineer the path. This is why modeling, rather than starting from scratch, is one of the fastest ways to grow. The smartest content creators don't try to invent from scratch. They study what's already working, figure out why it works, and then adapt the structure to fit their own voice, message, and brand. It's not copying, it's evolution. What most people overlook is this: Great content isn't improvised. It's patterned. It's repeatable. It's built with intention. And when you start thinking like a showrunner instead of just a poster, the entire game changes.

When you're analyzing successful content, break it down into two components.

Interest Topics are what the content is actually about. In fitness, this might be "fat loss" or "building muscle." In business, it could be "productivity hacks" or "leadership mistakes." Each interest topic has different audience appeal and viral potential.

Idea Formats are the repeatable structures that frame those topics. Think "$1 vs. $1,000 comparisons," "Give me 5 minutes and I'll show you . . ." tutorials, or "Things I wish I knew when I was 20" advice formats.

The most successful content combines proven interest topics with proven idea formats. Instead of guessing what will resonate, find topics that consistently perform in your niche then pair them with formats that have worked in adjacent spaces.

A winning idea format can become the foundation for an ongoing series. The format provides the consistency your audience recognizes, while rotating interest topics keeps each episode fresh. This is how you turn individual viral moments into sustainable content systems.

We live in an era where social media is the new television. TikTok, YouTube, and Instagram are the networks, and your phone is the screen we watch them on. These platforms aren't just apps anymore. They're channels. And the creator? You're not just posting content. You're the main character in a show people binge, follow, and share. The truth is, "social media" is a misnomer. What we're really talking about is personal television. Every creator is essentially running their own TV channel, complete with programming, recurring shows, and an audience that tunes in regularly. The difference is that instead of broadcasting to millions through a network, you're creating intimate, one-to-one connections that sometimes even feel as personal as a FaceTime call. Social-first shows aren't designed like the old shotgun approach where you're spraying content everywhere and hoping some of it hits people sitting on their couches. They're designed for personal connection. When someone watches your content, it doesn't feel like they're part of an audience of thousands. It feels like you're talking directly to them, in their living room, during their lunch break, or while they're getting ready for bed.

TV has always relied on formats, structured blueprints that turn ideas into consistent programming. Game shows. Talk shows. Skits. Monologues. Sitcoms. Now we're seeing that same DNA show up in the most successful social-first creators today. Let me show you what I mean:

- MrBeast turned game show dynamics into bingeable digital stunts that grab attention from the first second and reward it with massive payoffs.
- Erika Kullberg created a legal advice skit series where she plays both the consumer and the employee with signature phrases like, "Erika taught me. She's a lawyer and reads the fine print so I don't have to."
- Daniel Mac turned man on the street interviews into the new *MTV Cribs*. His viral catchphrase "What do you do for a living?" transformed luxury car sightings into bite-sized status tours.
- David Dobrik didn't just vlog, he built a personal sitcom. His friend group became recurring characters, his edits felt like punchlines, and his energy made every video feel like a chaotic group hang.

These creators didn't invent a completely new idea, but they did create a new way of doing it. They chose a proven format, added their own twist, and repeated it until it became unmistakably their own show.

THE MASS APPEAL RULE

To really understand why some content spreads and others flop, you have to look at how social media is built. Platforms prioritize keeping people satisfied so they stay on the platform longer and can be served more ads. While they do care about relevance, they ultimately reward content that generates strong engagement across broader interest groups, not just narrow customer segments.

This is why aiming only at your ideal customer profile puts a ceiling on your growth. In the real world, people do not consume content as isolated individuals. They consume it as members of groups. We see ourselves as parents, entrepreneurs, athletes, marketers, gamers, or fans. These identities overlap, and the more your content resonates across multiple groups, the further it can travel. Virality lives in those intersections.

Mass appeal does not mean trying to reach the general public. It does not mean watering down your message until it loses its power. Mass appeal means designing your content so it connects with big, relatable groups inside and around your niche. Think about Netflix's *Selling Sunset*. Realtors watch for strategies, affluent buyers tune in for the homes, and general viewers binge the drama. One show speaks to three different groups at once, which is why it became a global hit. This is what I mean by mass appeal within your niche: creating content that speaks to the broader ecosystem of people who orbit around your area of expertise

Your social media content works the same way. If you only satisfy your narrowest niche, the algorithm has no reason to push you further. But if you frame your message so it connects with larger identities and adjacent interests, you align with the platform's core incentive: maximize satisfaction across groups.

Now let's look at two examples of how my team and I applied the full approach we've discussed throughout this chapter with some of our clients.

1. Nikki Haskell: Borrowing a Proven Format to Create a Social-First Show

Remember the "grandfluencer" from the last chapter? When she wanted to break into digital content creation, she had no structured content strategy. She had decades of incredible experiences, stories, and insights as a prominent NYC socialite, but she lacked a clear format that would resonate with today's fast-paced social media audience. Instead of starting from scratch, we took a proven content format and made it uniquely hers.

We studied the success of the "Things I Wish I Knew" advice format, which many creators use to reflect on lessons they learned too late, and repositioned it to highlight Nikki's wealth of life experience. The result? "Things I Know in My 80s, That I Wish I Knew in My 20s"—a fresh, engaging take that stood out while still feeling familiar to audiences.

By turning this into a recognizable, repeatable format, we ensured that each post followed the same engaging structure, making it easy for people to consume, remember, and anticipate. This consistency played a key role in audience retention. Additionally, we positioned Nikki as a "grandfluencer," tapping into the rising trend of older influencers gaining traction online. This branding helped her stand out in a space often dominated by younger creators, giving her content a distinct identity.

The results were immediate. Nikki's content gained massive engagement, and she was featured on Australia's *Morning Show* as "America's grandfluencer," solidifying her status as a unique and credible voice in the digital space. The structured format gave her consistency, recognition, and authority, allowing her to turn her decades of experience into a compelling, shareable online presence.

Familiarity breeds trust. People naturally gravitate toward content structures they already recognize, but they engage with it when it has a fresh twist. By leveraging an existing, proven format and adapting it to Nikki's unique perspective, we were able to create something that felt both new and recognizable—ensuring it resonated deeply with her audience.

2. Non-Toxic Dad: Creating a Social-First Show for Health and Wellness Content

Warren Phillips had already established himself as "Non-Toxic Dad" with his passionate approach to educating families about toxic products.

He had built several thousand engaged followers who loved his practical advice, but he wanted to develop a more strategic approach to systematize his content for greater consistency and reach.

- **A grocery store toxic swaps format.** Warren's instinct to film in real shopping environments was already modeling the kind of content his audience craved, so we refined this into a signature format.

- **A signature hook: "[Product] is canceled!"** Warren had naturally developed this memorable hook, and we helped make it the centerpiece of his brand identity. Over time, this evolved into other variations, like "3 things I would never do as an environmental scientist" and "Is [product] toxic?"—all maintaining that same direct, curiosity-driven approach that made people stop scrolling.

- **Step-by-step education.** Warren always had a strong marketing background, but translating that into short-form video required a different approach. We worked together to channel his knowledge into the language of social media—creating visual hooks, bite-size insights, and supporting graphics that let the visuals do the heavy lifting instead of relying purely on explanation.

This systematic approach changed everything. By formalizing Warren's natural strengths into a repeatable structure, Non-Toxic Dad grew from several thousand followers to over 1 million, regularly achieving 30+ million views across all his channels. His engagement skyrocketed, and his brand became synonymous with approachable, practical health education, with health-conscious viewers now seeing him as their go-to expert.

You don't need to reinvent the wheel to make an impact. Find what works, adapt it to your niche, and deliver it consistently with your unique voice. When your audience knows what to expect and why they should keep coming back, you don't just gain followers—you build a movement.

WHY LONG-TERM IMPACT MATTERS MORE THAN VIRAL DOPAMINE HITS

Going viral once is luck. Staying relevant? That's strategy. Most people chase the dopamine hit. They post random content, hoping something takes off. And when it does, they think they've made it—until the attention fades and they're back at zero. But the experts who win long-term understand something deeper: One post might introduce you to the world. A ongoing show makes sure the world never forgets you.

Think about it. Kim Kardashian had *Keeping Up with the Kardashians*. Paris Hilton had *The Simple Life*. Oprah had *The Oprah Winfrey Show*. They didn't just build brands—they built media ecosystems. Each one used structured, repeatable content to train audiences to keep tuning in. Today's top content creators are doing the same thing, but they're doing it through podcasts, TikTok, Instagram, YouTube, with social-first formats that feel like TV made for your phone.

This isn't just a content strategy. It's neuroscience. A recurring show taps into long-term potentiation (LTP)—the brain's natural mechanism for memory formation. When your audience sees you showing up in the same style, tone, or structure again and again, their brain starts connecting the dots. You go from a video they saw once . . . to a person they remember. From a creator they follow . . . to an authority they trust.

That's the real game. Not just reach. ROAC: Return on Attention Created. Every post either builds your identity, increases trust, or adds leverage to your brand. If it doesn't do any of those things, it's just noise. So instead of chasing trends or throwing out content and hoping it sticks, ask yourself: What's the show I want to be known for? What's the feeling I want people to associate with me? And how can I repeat it until it becomes mine? When you find your format, and commit to it, everything changes. Not just your content. Your business. Your reputation. Your leverage. That's not just influence. That's legacy.

Chapter 12
ADAPT LIKE A DIGITAL NATIVE

It is not the strongest that survives; but the species that
survives is the one that is able best to adapt and adjust to
the changing environment in which it finds itself.

—Leon C. Megginson[11]

We don't just use the internet anymore. We live inside it. The digital world isn't
separate from the real world anymore. It's where business happens, relationships form, and culture is shaped in real time. Every day, people
spend an average of two hours and 23 minutes scrolling, swiping, and
engaging on social media. That's over a full month of screen time per
year.[12] But this isn't just passive consumption. What happens online now
dictates what happens offline, from careers and finances to relationships
and beyond.

Social media isn't just a tool or an app; it's an ecosystem, a living
environment with its own cultures, rules, and unspoken expectations. If

you don't understand these nuances, you'll always feel like an outsider. To thrive in this space, you need to do more than post content. You need to actually become part of the community.

Most experts treat social media like a billboard: Just throw your stuff up there and hope people notice. But that's not how this actually works. Digital natives see it differently. To them, these spaces aren't just for broadcasting, they're for participating.

So what does that mean for you as a creator? It means shifting your mindset from "posting content" to "adapting to digital culture." It means understanding the unique behaviors, language, and engagement dynamics of each platform so your content feels native, not forced.

This chapter will change how you see social media and show you how to stand out instead of just yelling into the void. Understanding this journey, this evolution from specialist to authority to guru, requires more than just tactics. It demands a fundamental shift in how you see yourself and your role in the world. Because in today's Creator Economy, success isn't about being loudest. It's about being deeply understood.

SEEING BEYOND THE OBVIOUS

Sunday mornings in my house had a ritual. While everyone else flipped through the newspaper for headlines, sports scores, or political updates, I had only one priority: the sales ads.

Every week, I'd rush to the mailbox, hoping to grab the paper before my dad. If I was too slow, I'd rip it from his hands and flip past the black-and-white pages, straight to the vibrant spreads from Fry's, Circuit City, and Best Buy.

Most people saw a mess of flyers and price lists. I saw possibility. A discounted graphics card wasn't just a deal, it was a chance to build a better gaming rig. A sale on joysticks? A new way to experience a game.

Each component, from memory cards to processors, was a step toward something bigger.

Even back then, I wasn't just consuming information—I was looking for opportunities, piecing together what others overlooked. And in today's digital world, that ability to see beyond the obvious is the difference between those who get lost in the noise and those who shape it.

DIGITAL NATIVES VS. DIGITAL IMMIGRANTS

Before we get into the practical stuff, let me explain the key difference between digital natives and digital immigrants.

A digital native is someone who grew up immersed in technology. They don't just play the game, they instinctively understand the rules because they grew up in this environment. They don't just use digital platforms, they instinctively understand them. They pick up trends fast, navigate online communities with ease, and adapt to new platforms without hesitation. To them, the internet isn't separate from real life. It's where life happens.

A digital immigrant, on the other hand, adopted technology later. They may have deep expertise in their field, but online spaces feel like a second language. Instead of effortlessly keeping up with digital trends, they often feel like they're playing catch-up, trying to decode shifting audience behaviors, platform algorithms, and engagement strategies.

If you're reading this, you likely fall somewhere along this spectrum. Maybe you're a millennial who remembers dial-up internet but adapted quickly to social media. Maybe you're Gen Z, for whom digital fluency is second nature. Or maybe you're a seasoned professional who has mastered your industry but is now trying to translate that expertise into the online world. Wherever you land, your success as a creator depends on one thing: your ability to adapt.

Take my 84-year-old client, Nikki Haskell. When she first joined
TikTok, it felt completely foreign. Fast-paced trends, short-form videos, meme-driven content—none of it matched the media landscape
she built her career in. But instead of resisting it, she embraced the
shift. With guidance from my team of digital natives, Nikki learned
the platform, adapted to its culture, and now racks up millions of
views every month.

The lesson? Anyone can learn to thrive in new digital spaces if they're
willing to observe, adapt, and engage.

Why Digital Natives See It Differently

Most people still see social media as a broadcast channel, a megaphone
to push out content, get engagement, and repeat. But that's an outdated
mindset. That's not how digital spaces actually work, and it's not how
digital natives see them.

For those who grew up online, platforms aren't just tools for promotion. They are environments where people live, interact, and shape culture in real time. Every scroll, every tap, every notification is part of an
intricate ecosystem that's woven into everyday life. The more integrated
these platforms become, the more they blur the lines between the digital
and the physical world, influencing not just what we consume but how
we think, how we connect, and how we make decisions.

This may sound extreme at first, but think about it practically:
How many times a day do you have a thought, type it into a search
bar or AI chatbot, and instantly get an answer? Need a recipe? Directions? A product recommendation? A psychological analysis of your
ex's latest text message? Within seconds, the answer appears. We don't
even question it anymore. It's so seamless, so automatic, that we take
it for granted.

But what if the answer appeared before you even searched for it?

This isn't some futuristic concept. It's already happening. The internet has transformed from a static collection of pages into a predictive ecosystem where algorithms don't just respond to behavior—they anticipate it. Platforms track everything: your searches, your clicks, the content you linger on, even the videos you almost watch but scroll past at the last second. They don't wait for you to seek out information, they serve it to you before you even know you need it.

I used to make fun of my parents for the way things worked in their time. In India, families would place classified ads in newspapers to arrange marriages, listing details like education, family status, and income. To me, that always seemed ridiculous, outdated, and transactional. Why would anyone find a life partner through an ad in a newspaper?

But today, most relationships are found the exact same way.

Only now, instead of flipping through newspaper ads, we swipe through dating profiles, ranked and sorted by algorithms. Instead of newspaper editors curating a handful of options, AI-driven platforms analyze billions of data points to match people based on location, preferences, and engagement patterns. The logic hasn't changed, just the efficiency of the system.

And it's not just dating. Jobs, shopping, entertainment, friendships—everything has moved from "search-based" to "match-based." You no longer need to find things. Things find you.

Want a job? AI-powered platforms don't wait for you to apply, they suggest roles based on your behavior, skills, and search history. Need help? Chat-based AI assistants are ready to analyze your mood, recommend a therapist, or even suggest the next book you should read. Looking for new friends? Social apps like Bumble introduce you to people algorithmically, the same way dating apps do.

This is the world digital natives understand instinctively. They don't just use platforms, they exist inside them. They navigate digital spaces the way previous generations navigated cities, with an understanding of their culture, flow, and unspoken rules.

THE DIGITAL LANDSCAPE HAS CHANGED

What most people do wrong is that they see social media as just a marketing tool, a place to post content, attract followers, and drive engagement. But digital natives see it differently: We view platforms as entire digital nations, each with their own culture, customs, and unspoken rules. Just like traveling to a foreign country, if you want to connect with the people, you have to understand and respect their way of life.

The mistake many creators make? They post the same content across multiple platforms without adapting it to fit the culture of each space. For example, posting random quotes might be perfectly acceptable on Facebook, but on TikTok, it would feel out of place. Congratulating a colleague on a promotion wouldn't make sense on YouTube, but on LinkedIn, it's expected.

Sure, some cultural overlap may exist, meaning the same content sometimes can naturally perform well across multiple platforms. TikTok videos often do great as Instagram Reels or YouTube Shorts. But don't see this as a free pass for you to go ahead and just start copying and pasting everything across platforms without tweaking it. A strategic crossover is totally possible, but it needs to be intentional. That's why it's so smart to have a recurring show. When your content follows a recognizable structure or format, it becomes easier to remix across platforms. You can spin it into carousels, turn it into a graphic, slice it into shorter clips, or expand it into a longer thread—without losing clarity or brand identity. But to make it work, you still need to respect the nuances of each platform, put on your digital native hat, and speak the language of the feed.

HOW TO NAVIGATE THE DIGITAL WORLD AS AN EXPERT

If you're a digital native, you probably do this instinctively. You scroll TikTok and immediately pick up on the latest trends. You know how to adjust your tone for different platforms. You get the humor, the inside jokes, the references.

If you're a digital immigrant, it might take some time. You may find yourself wondering why certain posts perform better than others, or why an audience doesn't respond the way you expected. That's normal.

So how do you bridge the gap? It starts with observation.

Instead of rushing to post, spend time immersing yourself in the platform. Watch how people engage, what kinds of posts get shared, and how trends evolve. TikTok isn't LinkedIn, and X isn't Instagram. Every platform has its own language.

Then, engage in ways that feel native. Don't just drop content and disappear. Comment. Stitch. Duet. Join conversations that are already happening instead of trying to force your own. Be a participant, not just a broadcaster.

Once you understand the landscape, adapt your messaging for each platform. The same insight that works in a long-form LinkedIn post won't translate to a 10-second TikTok. A post on X doesn't work as an Instagram caption. Tailor your content for the space you're in.

And finally, stay curious. The internet moves fast. What worked yesterday may not work tomorrow. Trends shift. Algorithms evolve. The best creators aren't the ones who mastered a single formula; they're the ones who continuously experiment, learn, and refine their approach.

Because in a world where digital serendipity (thanks to the power of the algorithm) feels effortless and instant, shaping what we see, the ones who understand how to align with it will always have the advantage.

SERENDIPITY ENGINES, OR HOW
PLATFORMS ENGINEER DISCOVERY

Admit it, you've probably joked, "Is my phone spying on me?" after an ad or video pops up that's uncannily relevant. But the truth? It's not magic or mind reading, it's an advanced algorithm that tracks your clicks, likes, searches, and even how long you linger on certain posts, whether you pause a video, and even how fast you scroll past certain content. What feels like serendipity to you is actually the result of data science working at lightning speed to anticipate your interests and deliver content that feels tailor-made for you.

Rather than viewing algorithms as rigid lines of code, think of them as serendipity engines, intentionally crafted to create moments of discovery that feel spontaneous but are anything but random. Instead of merely responding to your searches, they anticipate your interests, showing you content that gets you engaged before you even realize you're looking for it.

It starts with tracking behavior. Not just what you click on but what you linger on, what you almost engage with but scroll past at the last second, and even how long you hover over a post before deciding to move on. Over time, patterns emerge, clustering people into interest spaces where similar behaviors and preferences align. If you've been watching a string of Italian cooking videos, the algorithm notices that others with the same habit are also engaging with soccer-related content. Without you asking, soccer clips start appearing in your feed, not because you searched for them but because the system recognizes an invisible link between your interests and those of millions of others.

So how can you take advantage of these serendipity engines? Don't just create content, align with what people are already searching for. When your content naturally fits into an existing interest space, algorithms are more likely to surface it organically, leading to faster growth without relying on ads or random chance.

At the same time, let's be real: No matter how well you optimize your content, some things will always be out of your control. Sometimes algorithms aren't just matching content to user behavior; they are working toward their own platform goals, whether that's keeping people engaged longer, maximizing ad revenue, or pushing certain trends.

Another thing platforms love? Experimenting. They constantly test new content placements, slipping unexpected posts into users' feeds just to gauge reactions. If enough people engage, they'll amplify that type of content even further. While this is another one of those things that you can't control, it actually works in your favor, because even if your content isn't an exact match for someone's past behavior, the algorithm might still push it if it aligns with what the platform is prioritizing at the time.

CREATING CONTENT THAT MEETS REAL NEEDS

Beyond algorithmic discovery, there's another powerful way to grow as a creator, and that is by tapping into life effects: those moments when people aren't just passively consuming content but actively searching for a solution.

A parent who throws out their back while playing with their kids isn't scrolling mindlessly anymore—they're urgently looking for a chiropractor. A college student struggling with procrastination doesn't just watch random productivity hacks—they type "how to be more productive" into YouTube, searching for real answers. A small business owner, realizing their online presence is weak, isn't aimlessly browsing—they're actively looking up "how to grow on Instagram."

These are the moments that drive real engagement, when people need answers, not entertainment. If your content provides a timely solution, you're not just gaining a view. You're earning trust. And by creating content that anticipates these life effects, you're positioning yourself as a valuable resource exactly when people need help the most, providing content that is immediate, relevant, and actionable.

That is why this approach doesn't just attract an audience, it builds credibility. When people see that you genuinely understand their struggles and offer real solutions, they'll keep coming back. In the long run, solving real problems is both good content strategy and the foundation for a loyal, engaged community.

THE FUTURE BELONGS TO THE ADAPTABLE

Adapting to digital culture is an important part of the Guru's Journey in today's world. The authorities who thrive aren't necessarily the most technically savvy, they're the ones who understand that mastering digital spaces requires the same internal flexibility they've developed in their expertise. Platforms change, algorithms shift, and new trends emerge daily. But one thing remains constant: The experts who succeed are the ones who adapt.

Becoming a sought-after guru isn't about mastering one platform or one strategy—it's about learning to navigate digital spaces with fluency, creativity, and cultural awareness.

If you're a *digital native*, lean into your instinctive understanding of digital culture—but don't neglect strategy and depth. Having an eye for trends is great, but true authority comes from expertise and thought leadership.

If you're a *digital immigrant*, leverage your experience and industry knowledge—but don't resist adapting to new digital formats. Your expertise is valuable, but it needs to be translated into the right language for online audiences.

So, whether you're stepping into social media for the first time or refining an already strong presence, remember: Your success isn't just about what you know. It's about how well you adapt.

Chapter 13

THE PERSONAL MEDIA COMPANY MODEL

The whole is greater than the sum of its parts.

—Aristotle

In 2020, the world hit pause. COVID-19 lockdowns forced everyone into a surreal state of stillness, and like so many others, I was stuck inside, desperately looking for ways to stay sane. One day, during another routine trip to Target to hoard toilet paper (jk, I just wanted to make sure you were still reading), I wandered into the toy aisle and spotted something familiar that I hadn't seen in decades, since a time when life was so much simpler. Staring me in the face was the rainbow coloration of the nerdiest toy on planet Earth: a Rubik's Cube. It instantly took me on a stroll down memory lane. That weird, subtle mix of nostalgia and frustration settled in my stomach. I remember as a child that I never had the patience to solve it. But what about now? I had all the time in the world on my hands, since Los Angeles was in full lockdown mode. So while everyone else was binge-watching the Netflix escapades of the Tiger King and his archnemesis, Carol Baskin, I began devoting myself to the challenge of solving this childhood puzzle.

At first, it was just a game, one I wanted to win. So I went online and started studying patterns, memorizing algorithms, and even experimenting with solving it while microdosing LSD-25 to be like Steve Jobs (yes, really). But as I became obsessed with cracking the code, something else clicked in my brain. This new obsession with the Rubik's Cube became about something more than just solving a puzzle. That cube was the perfect metaphor for how I helped clients solve the puzzle of their own brand ecosystem.

Let me explain.

THE PUZZLE OF A DIGITAL BRAND

The Rubik's Cube taught me something huge about building a brand: Everything affects everything else. You can't focus on growing your Instagram and ignore your email list. You can't perfect your website while neglecting your content strategy. Just like the cube, when you change one thing, it messes with everything else. Solving just one side doesn't cut it. You need all the colors working in harmony. You can't keep fiddling with one side (one platform) and expect the rest to magically fall into place. Every shift impacts the whole cube. That's why building a business is so hard. If the pieces don't fit together, everything falls apart.

And yet, that's exactly how most people approach their online presence. They focus on one thing in isolation (maybe that's growing their Instagram, selling a course, or launching a podcast) without ever realizing how that will affect their brand as a whole. It's as if they are celebrating solving one side of the cube, only to turn it around and see that the rest is consequently jumbled.

Suddenly, the Rubik's Cube wasn't just a toy anymore. I saw it as a blueprint for something I'd been unsuccessfully trying to articulate to clients for years. Over the course of my career, I had helped experts and thought leaders turn their expertise into thriving businesses, but every time, I'd struggled to find the right words on how the different pieces fit together and why they should be looking at the bigger picture, not just at its parts in isolation. Now, it was staring me right in the face in the form of my favorite childhood toy: a Rubik's Cube.

THE METHOD BEHIND THE MADNESS

With the Rubik's Cube, there's a right way to solve it. You don't just randomly twist and turn, hoping for the best (like little AJ back in the day). There's a system, a step-by-step process that requires patience and precision. Just like with the Rubik's Cube, the real game isn't solving the puzzle; it's learning how to orchestrate every move so that each move brings us closer to our final goal.

The reason that pesky little plastic cube is so annoying to novices is that they think it's dumb luck and random twists and turns that will get them the outcome they desire. Little do people know, but a Rubik's Cube has over 43 quintillion possible combinations—more than there are grains of sand on all the beaches on Earth—yet any scrambled cube can be solved in 20 moves or less with the right method. That's why random moves never work. The answer lies in taking calculated steps in a formulaic approach in the right order at the right time.

I remember when I solved the Rubik's Cube for the very first time. I am pretty sure my neighbors heard me yelling for my brother, Jason, out of pure excitement. It felt like that scene in *The Pursuit of Happyness* when Will Smith's character solves the Rubik's Cube in the back of the cab to impress the boss.

Just as the Rubik's Cube has proven methods, so does building your brand. Here's what I discovered.

1. First Layer: Lay the Foundations, Capture Attention, and Build Trust

First, you solve the bottom layer. For the personal brand you're building, that means discovering what actually resonates and developing your unique content approach. This is the phase where you experiment, share your expertise, and pilot different formats to find your creative lane. Maybe it's short-form skits where you play two characters to explain complex ideas. Maybe it's long-form interviews, or behind-the-scenes vlogs where you document your journey building in public. The point isn't to go viral right away, it's to find what feels authentic to you and delivers real value to others. Think of it like a TV network testing shows. Most shows don't make it, but the ones that do become the foundation of the network. That's your goal here: to find the format, the rhythm, the perspective that makes people say, "I need more of this." Because without that foundational content strategy, without a repeatable, resonant way to show up, your entire brand ecosystem falls apart. This is where it all begins.

You may be thinking, *But AJ, how do I know if my content is actually working?*

That is when the challenge really starts.

2. Second Layer: Start Monetizing Without Breaking the System

This is where you get intentional about what's working. Just like solving the middle layer of a Rubik's Cube, you have to make strategic moves without dismantling what you've already built.

The signals are usually clear, and they all point to your ROAC: Return on Attention Created. Yes, the engagement numbers matter. Comments, shares, saves, DMs are the signs people are paying attention.

But they're just one part of the bigger picture. What really tells you your show is working is when attention turns into real impact. Are people trying out your advice? Tagging you in their wins? Sending messages about how your content solved a real problem? Are other experts starting to reference your work or invite you into their world? These stories of transformation, combined with consistent engagement, tell you that your show isn't just getting seen, it's creating value. And that's when everything shifts. You're no longer just posting. You're building a business around proven resonance. Passion fuels the creativity, but strategy turns it into something sustainable.

This isn't 2010. We're past the point of questioning whether people support creators they trust. They do. Every day, your audience is buying, signing up, and investing in solutions. The only question is—are they doing it with you, or with someone else? But here's what most experts miss: Unless your products or services feel organic, you don't monetize during the show, you monetize during the commercial breaks. Your organic content builds the audience and authority. Your paid ads, targeted at people who've already consumed your content, handle the selling. When someone sees your ad after watching your show for weeks, it's not an interruption, it's a recommendation from someone they already trust. Once you accept that your social presence has real business potential, everything changes. You start building systems, optimizing for consistency, and tracking actual impact, not just views. You stop treating this like a hobby that might pay off someday, and start running it like a media company that deserves professional treatment.

The challenge? Making that transition without breaking the trust you've built. Push too hard toward monetizing your airtime, and you become just another influencer hawking products. Don't invest enough, and your brand never evolves beyond expensive content production. The goal is to find that sweet spot—where your business growth actually enhances the value you provide.

3. Third Layer: Creating an Experience for Your Audience

Once your show is proven and your business engine is running, you enter the next evolution, the moment where everything starts to scale. The first two layers were about finding your hit show and building the business around it. This third layer is about expansion. You're no longer just running a show, you're building a full network experience.

At this stage, you're not just making content or selling your offers. You're franchising your personal brand. Your show becomes the anchor, spinning off into companion series, other platform-specific formats, and fresh creative concepts. If you started with short-form, now you're developing long-form content. If you began with long-form, you're designing original concepts made for short-form content. Insights become carousel graphics. Stories are transformed into animated clips with a cartoon character of yourself. Case studies evolve into engaging email series. You show up in livestreams, podcasts, AI-generated content, and whatever format your audience is obsessed with next. You're no longer just showing up, you're building a branded universe with multiple entry points, just like a media franchise.

This is where you shift from getting attention to owning it. Think of Alex Hormozi, Gary Vaynerchuk, or Mel Robbins. You see them everywhere—on Google, Instagram, LinkedIn, podcasts. Each social media channel has different shows, but they all reinforce the same core identity. They become the go-to voice in their space. That's not accidental, it's programming. It's network thinking.

This is the power of Layer 3. You're not just someone people follow, you're someone they trust. When they have a problem, they think of your content. When they're scrolling, they stop at your face. When they're making decisions, they hear your voice in their head. "What would Hormozi do?" "What would Mel Robbins do?" "What would Gary Vee do?" Your presence moves from casual to constant. Your content, products, message, and community now work together like a connected lineup of shows on the same channel. Each one reinforces your expertise until you're not just relevant, you're indispensable. People don't just consume your content. They subscribe to your entire world. That's when you've built something that lasts.

SEEING THE BIGGER PICTURE

There's a scene in the biopic *Steve Jobs* where Jobs says, "Musicians play their instruments. I play the orchestra." That line stuck with me because it perfectly describes the digital world today: a massive, interconnected symphony of platforms, content, and people.

Think about it. The instruments in this digital orchestra are keyboards, smartphones, cameras, software, and automation tools. The musicians? They're the team of specialists, the content creators, creative directors, social media managers, producers, video editors, copywriters, marketers, graphic designers, web developers, data analysts, and strategists.

And don't forget the most important part: the audience. They're the ones scrolling through social media, opening emails, listening to podcasts, reading blogs, watching videos, or engaging in online communities, ravenously eating up all your online content. In the digital world, each platform is like a different channel in your personal media network. Your job as the conductor is to make sure each one delivers a consistent and compelling performance that keeps your audience engaged and asking for an encore.

What I've learned from both the Rubik's Cube and years of digital marketing is that real success comes from understanding the relationships between all these moving parts. Every post, every offer, every interaction is connected. When experts understand this and are able to orchestrate their digital marketing correctly, one thing is for sure: They end up creating something far greater than the sum of its parts.

CONTENT, COMMERCE, AND CONCERT

The truth is, I had been using this approach with my clients for years, trying to explain to them why each and every part of their presence was important. I just hadn't put a name to it. And then that fateful day in my neighborhood Target gave me the bullseye I'd been waiting for. Somewhere between the mountain of Clorox wipes, Purell hand sanitizer, and extra-soft toilet paper was that lonely Rubik's Cube, begging me to solve the riddle. And just like that, I realized what those three layers I'd been referencing actually represented: content, commerce, and concert—the three essential elements of every successful Personal Media Company.

1. Content: The Music That Draws People In

This is what captures people's attention. It's your voice, your message, your ability to provide value. Whether through videos, blog posts, podcasts, or social media, content is how you attract an audience and build trust. Without content, there's no audience, no engagement, and no foundation to grow on.

2. Commerce: The Merch Booth That Converts Fans into Customers

Commerce is where attention turns into revenue. If you're only focused on creating content but not on monetizing it, it means you're running on an unsustainable model. On the contrary, if you push sales too hard without real value attached, your audience will most probably tune out.

So what's the secret here, AJ?

The secret is to monetize in a way that feels natural. How? By leading people off social media and into environments you can control, like your email list, sales pages, memberships, or exclusive communities. It's more or less the same job as that of a concierge guiding concertgoers from the music hall to the merch booth. Not through pressure but because they genuinely want to complement their experience.

3. Concert: The Experience That Keeps People Coming Back

The magic happens when everything works together. The concert isn't just about what's happening in the moment, it's about creating an experience people remember so they keep showing up.

In your brand, this means orchestrating two distinct but connected experiences: the show and the commercial. Your organic content—your social-first show—builds momentum and guides your audience through a journey of trust and authority. Your paid advertising, the commercials, monetizes that trust by reaching people who already know your work. The magic happens when these work together: Your content makes your ads more valuable, and your ads scale what your content has already proven. Remember, you're not chasing one-time transactions; you're working to create a self-sustaining ecosystem where your audience feels connected, engaged, and eager to stay involved. When content and commerce work together through your concert experience, they build more than revenue. They establish your identity as the go-to authority in your space, deepen trust with your audience, and create leverage for partnerships, speaking opportunities, and bigger deals that wouldn't be possible otherwise. Instead of focusing on getting your prospects to pay you once, focus on helping them grow and evolve by consistently solving their pain points over time. This will add real, tangible value.

The beauty of this system is its self-reinforcing nature. Once it starts running, it creates a flywheel effect, in which each element strengthens the others, building momentum with every turn. This creates a special type of synergy that feels like magic to your raving fans. Your content fuels your community. Your community drives commerce. And your commerce funds even better content. The more you make, the more you can reinvest in production, marketing, and promoting the growth of your brand.

OK AJ, this sounds great in theory, but how do you actually do all this?

THINK LIKE A MEDIA EXECUTIVE

Now here's how you actually build this. You need to stop thinking like a content creator and start thinking like a media executive. I know that sounds intimidating, but hear me out. The most successful gurus don't just post content, they program it. They create shows, series, and systematic content that builds anticipation and keeps audiences coming back, just like your favorite TV network. Remember how I mentioned that social media is the new television? Well, if that's true, then you're not just a performer, you're the network. You're the producer. You're the talent. And most importantly, you're the one calling the shots about what gets made and when it airs.

This changes how you think about everything. Instead of just posting random stuff and crossing your fingers, you start being strategic about what you put out there. You stop playing the game blindly and start making calculated moves that build toward your bigger goals. You build shows that people anticipate. You develop content that creates appointment viewing, even if that "appointment" is someone opening TikTok during their lunch break. But here's the media executive secret: Your organic programming isn't just building an audience—it's making your advertising inventory more valuable. Every person who watches your show becomes a warmer lead for your commercials—those targeted ads that reach people who already know your work. This is how real media companies operate: The programming builds the audience, the commercials monetize it. But here's the thing. You can't just jump into running a full media company overnight. Just like solving that Rubik's Cube, there's a progression. A system. And that system mirrors exactly what I saw working with clients and other successful content creators on social media.

So how do you actually build this Personal Media Company step by step? You follow a four-stage development system that mirrors how real media companies create hit shows. Each stage builds on the last, and if you skip one, you'll struggle to replicate what's working because you never learned the fundamentals. Here's exactly how to build your Personal Media Company from scratch.

Stage 1: Proof of Concept—Your Creative Laboratory

Think of this stage like a TV network's pilot season. Every year, networks spend millions testing new show concepts, knowing most will flop. But the ones that don't? They become the foundation of the network's identity. That's exactly what you're doing here. You're not trying to create the perfect show right out of the gate. You're experimenting. You're testing. You're figuring out what resonates with your audience before you commit significant time and energy.

When I worked with Nikki Haskell, we didn't start with her "signature advice in my 80s" format. We tested everything—celebrity stories, product reviews, lifestyle content. But when we hit on that simple concept of "things I know in my 80s that I wish I knew in my 20s," we knew we had something. The engagement was immediate. The comments were passionate. People were tagging their friends. That's your signal. When you find content that makes people stop scrolling, engage deeply, and share organically, you've found your proof of concept.

Your mission in this stage: Test three to five different content formats to share your expertise. Use existing structures that already work. Don't try to reinvent the wheel. Choose one or two platforms as your testing ground, but don't be afraid to post multiple variations to see what clicks. The beauty of this stage? It requires minimal investment. You're not hiring teams or buying expensive equipment. You're just experimenting with your phone and your expertise, seeing what combination creates magic.

Stage 2: Pilot Phase—Testing Winning Concepts

Once you've found something that clicks in Stage 1, you're no longer experimenting randomly. Now you're piloting it like a real series. In traditional TV, a pilot is just one episode. But in the social media world, a single video isn't enough to prove staying power. That's why your Pilot Phase means producing three to five episodes using the same format, with consistent structure, tone, and delivery. The goal is to see if the concept holds up when repeated and if your audience starts to recognize and return for your content.

You're not fully developing the show yet. You're pressure-testing it as a small batch of episodes: Can you replicate the success? Can you hold attention over multiple episodes? Can you start building pattern recognition with your audience? When Netflix greenlights a show, they don't just commit to one episode. They order a season. They double down on the concept, but only if the pilot proves it's worth the investment. You're doing the same thing here. This is the point where your audience starts to see you not just as someone who had a great idea . . . but someone worth subscribing to.

I'll never forget watching Nikki Haskell's content evolve during this phase. We'd identified that her "wisdom from the 80s" format was working, but the real breakthrough came when we started adding consistent elements. From her signature phrases, her visual style, and even the way she delivered her punchlines. Suddenly, people weren't just watching random videos from an interesting older woman. They were watching Nikki's Show.

Your mission in this stage: Create three to five episodes of your winning concept. Develop your recurring elements like catchphrases, visual consistency, intro style. This is where you test for early signs of pattern recognition. You're not aiming for perfection or full branding yet, just enough consistency to see if the format has legs. If people engage across multiple episodes and start responding to the same style, that's your signal to move forward.

Stage 3: Show Development—Building Trust Through Consistency
Now that your pilot format is working, it's time to commit. This is where you shift from testing mode to trust-building mode. Think of this as

your breakout season. You've got an audience that's interested—now you earn their loyalty. This is where you lock in your creative style. You establish pattern recognition. You make your content feel like a ritual.

When Gary Vaynerchuk was building *Wine Library TV*, he didn't just make random wine videos. He created a show. Same intro every time. Same energy. Same format. People knew what to expect, and that familiarity bred trust. That trust became authority. And that authority became millions in revenue. And it's not just long-form creators doing this. Erika Kullberg's short-form legal explainers follow a simple, repeatable format: two characters and a surprising insight. Same tone. Same delivery. Same setup. Daniel Mac's street interviews are instantly recognizable: the opening line, the pacing, the payoff. That repeatability builds expectation, and expectation builds loyalty.

The goal of Stage 3 is audience retention. People should start knowing what to expect from you—and look forward to it. That familiarity becomes trust, and that trust is what drives long-term audience growth and authority. This is also when you can start testing light monetization. You now have an audience that knows your voice and trusts your expertise. Sometimes your offers fit naturally into your content—like demonstrating a tool you actually use or offering a free resource that solves the exact problem you just discussed. Maybe it's a checklist, template, or mini-course that extends the value of what they just learned. Simple automated systems can capture their interest in the moment and guide them into your email list where deeper relationships develop. You're not selling to strangers—you're serving an audience that already values what you bring. Your show has already done the trust-building, so basic monetization feels like a natural next step rather than an interruption.

Your mission in this stage: Commit fully to your winning format and start building repetition into your content. Focus on making each episode feel like "must-watch" material. Something your audience looks forward to before it even drops. This is also the point where you begin developing simple backend workflows to streamline production and marketing, and maintain consistency. You're shifting from being just a content creator to running your operation like a media company.

Stage 4: Series Scaling—From Creator to Brand Ecosystem

Stage 3 was about building consistency and testing monetization. Stage 4 is about scaling everything systematically. This is where your advertising becomes exponentially more valuable—you're retargeting people who already know your work across multiple platforms and formats. Your organic content has created such strong brand recognition that your ads perform like recommendations from a trusted friend rather than cold sales pitches. Your brand begins to operate in layers, with flagship shows, spin-off formats, long-form and short-form content, and evergreen assets alongside timely responses. You're not just serving one type of audience anymore; you're programming different series to reach different segments across platforms.

Look at someone like Alex Hormozi. He doesn't just post random business tips. He's built an entire brand ecosystem: short-form videos that drive awareness, long-form videos and podcasts that deepen trust, email sequences that convert, books that anchor his authority—all reinforcing the same identity while serving different touchpoints in the audience journey.

The goal of Stage 4 is monetization at scale. This goes beyond ad revenue or brand deals. You're building multiple revenue streams, advanced automation sequences, and retargeting campaigns that all tie directly into your brand identity—from courses, digital products, consulting offers, to partnerships, licensing, and community-led programs. Every piece of content isn't just building trust; it's building leverage.

At this stage, your mission is to develop multiple shows or series under one unified brand umbrella. You'll need to grow your team and build backend systems that let you repurpose, distribute, and scale efficiently. Each format should be mapped to a clear business outcome, whether it's audience growth, lead generation, or direct sales. You're no longer just a creator. You're a media company with personality-driven programming, and your content now works for you, even when you sleep.

A DIGITAL SYMPHONY

Here's what most people miss: Content isn't just about going viral, it's about building a system that earns trust at scale, and then turning that trust into leverage. Each stage of the process plays a critical role. Stage 1 gives you traction. Stage 2 gives you recognition. Stage 3 gives you authority. And Stage 4 gives you freedom, because now your content isn't just performing, it's working for you, generating opportunity, income, and influence even when you're not online. When your media company is built right, content doesn't just get views, it gets results. That's how you move from chasing algorithms to owning attention.

But here's what most people get wrong about building a personal brand: They try to do everything at once. They want the polished production of Stage 4 with the budget of Stage 1. They want the systematic processes of an established media company without doing the testing required to know what actually works. But just like with the Rubik's Cube, you have to solve it layer by layer. Each stage builds on the previous one. Each phase teaches you something you'll need for the next level. When you follow this progression, something magical happens. Your content stops feeling random and starts feeling intentional. Your audience stops casually following you and starts actively anticipating your next post. Your monetization stops being opportunistic and starts being systematic. You transform from someone who creates content into someone who owns a media company. And in today's Creator Economy, that's the difference between making a living and building wealth.

Building this kind of integrated presence isn't easy. It's like solving a Rubik's Cube blindfolded—every move has to be deliberate and well thought out. But when the pieces align, something magical happens. Your content draws in attention, your commerce turns that attention into revenue, and your concert—the harmony of content and commerce—creates a lasting community.

It all brings us back to that moment of me in Target, holding a Rubik's Cube. What seemed like a simple lockdown distraction turned out to be a profound metaphor for digital brand building. Just as every master puzzle solver knows that success comes from understanding patterns, success in the digital world comes from understanding how all the pieces fit together. Every piece affects every other piece. Your Personal Media Company works the same way. Your proof of concept informs your pilot. Your pilot shapes your show. Your show evolves into a series. And your series becomes your empire. Each stage builds on the last, creating something far greater than the sum of its parts. That's the power of thinking like a media company. You're not just playing the content game—you're programming the entire experience.

Chapter 14

BREAKING THE *VOLT*

In the center of "belief" lies a "lie."

—Anonymous

Think back to your teenage years. Remember when anything felt possible? You weren't just dreaming of success; you were certain of it. If you wanted to be a rock star, you weren't fantasizing about playing local dive bars—you were headlining sold-out arenas. If you dreamed of being an athlete, you didn't picture yourself warming the bench—you saw yourself making history! If you were anything like me, you'd be in the driveway at sunset, counting down the final seconds, imagining the crowd erupting as you hit the game-winning three at the buzzer—NBA Finals, Game 7.

Then, life happened. In game terms, you hit your first major block.

Maybe you had a setback that shook your confidence. Maybe someone you admired told you to "be realistic." Or maybe—without even realizing it—you started absorbing the mindset of those around you, people who had already given up on their own dreams.

Little by little, your big dreams got infected. You caught *VOLT—the Virus of Limited Thinking*.

THE INVISIBLE CHAINS OF LIMITED THINKING

VOLT is highly contagious and can infect you in a single conversation. VOLT represents the biggest block in this game. Everyone worries about algorithms and competition, but the real battle is in your head. One negative comment can get entrenched in your nervous system and live stored in your cells for decades. It spreads like a virus through people who have already succumbed to it—those who have internalized their own limitations and now project them onto others.

VOLT spreads in places where negativity and fear are just normal. It's passed down through:

- Parents who, out of fear, teach their children to "play it safe."
- Friends who discourage bold ideas because they can't see them for themselves.
- Teachers, mentors, or bosses who unintentionally impose their own limitations on others.

And here's the scary part: Most people don't even know they've caught it. They think their limited thinking is just how things are. They believe the ceilings imposed on them by others are immovable, when in fact they are nothing more than inherited mental blocks.

HOW VOLT SPREADS

Imagine landing your dream job—you're excited, ambitious, ready to make an impact. You walk in on your first day, full of ideas and energy. But then, during your first coffee break, you overhear your colleagues talking about how things *really* work. "No one gets promoted here." "It's all about politics." "Merit doesn't matter."

At first, you dismiss it. *That won't be me.* You believe you'll be different. But as the days go by, you hear the same sentiments, over and over. Slowly, doubt creeps in. The bold vision you had for your career starts to fade. Without even realizing it, you begin to lower your expectations—to settle.

And just like that, you've caught VOLT.

This is how most people give up—not because they suck, but because they start believing other people's limitations as their own.

The real danger of VOLT isn't that it makes you less capable—it's that it convinces you to stop believing in your own potential. It doesn't weaken your skills or intelligence; it goes straight for that part of you that once saw no limits. The part that, as a teenager, dreamed freely and without hesitation. And once that belief fades, the symptoms start creeping in, and they show up everywhere:

- **Self-Doubt:** *Who am I to do this?*
- **Fear of Failure:** *What if I try and then embarrass myself?*
- **Imposter Syndrome:** *I'm not as good as people think I am.*
- **Playing Small:** *I should just be grateful for what I have.*
- **Avoidance of Responsibility:** *It's not my fault things are this way.*
- **Seeking External Validation:** *If people approve of me, I must be on the right path.*

The problem? The longer you're exposed to VOLT, the stronger its grip becomes. It weakens your ability to dream, dulls your ambition, and quickly leaves you with a potentially lifelong chronic handicap: a limited mindset.

ESCAPING THE "BEGINNER" LABEL

I've felt it too. Even when you think you're immune, even when you know you're capable of more, those outside limitations can creep in and shape your reality. Let me share a personal story that proves just how sneaky VOLT can be.

My high school had just built a state-of-the-art, million-dollar swimming pool, and I was thrilled. I considered myself a strong swimmer, and this was my chance to prove it. Then came first-period PE class. The water was freezing—so cold it took my breath away. One by one, we had to swim across the pool, demonstrating our skills. When my turn came, I gave it my all, channeling everything I had learned from summers spent at the local pool.

As I reached the other side, still gasping from the icy water, I heard my teacher yelling: "Look at me! Look at me! Go to group one for beginners!"

Beginner? Me? I was stunned, humiliated—even a little angry.

But here's the thing: I refused to accept it. The moment the teacher turned away, I swam under the lane dividers and quietly joined the advanced group. No one noticed. I trained with them for the rest of the semester. And you know what? I kept up. I belonged there.

That moment stuck with me for years—not because of what happened in that pool but because of what happened in my mind.

The truth is that even after proving myself in my career—after working with billionaires, celebrities, and Fortune 500 companies through my agency work—I still had moments when I felt like I had snuck into the advanced group. Like I didn't really belong.

That's what VOLT does to you. It convinces you that, no matter how far you've come, you're just not good enough. It whispers that you're just faking it—that it's only a matter of time before someone figures out you don't actually deserve your success. How do you overcome it? You have to reject it. Not by waiting for someone to validate you but by deciding that you belong. And then? You act like it.

THE THREE STAGES OF BELIEF

Your mindset is the foundation of everything you create: your success, your influence, your personal brand. But what if the way you think is secretly sabotaging your potential? One of the most powerful insights I ever got came from my mentor Roy: There are three belief systems running your life—limited beliefs, limiting beliefs, and limitless beliefs. To cure VOLT, you have to stop thinking with the first two . . . and start living from the third.

1. Limited Beliefs: The Invisible Chains

That's just the way things are.

People like me don't get those kinds of opportunities.

Success is for the lucky, not for me.

Limited beliefs are the deepest and most ingrained. These aren't just thoughts you have about yourself—they're the "truths" you've accepted about the world. The worst part? You don't even realize you're operating under them because they feel like reality.

Think about someone who grew up in a struggling household, constantly hearing, "Money doesn't grow on trees," or "We're just not the kind of people who get rich." Over time, that belief embeds itself so deeply that even when opportunities arise, they dismiss them without a second thought. The idea of financial success isn't even within reach, because they've accepted the "truth" that it's unattainable for them.

Symptoms of Limited Beliefs

- You don't question the status quo—you assume things are just *how they are.*
- You dismiss success as something meant for "other" people.
- You rarely, if ever, consider pursuing something beyond your perceived reach.

2. Limiting Beliefs: The Self-Inflicted Ceiling

I want to be successful, but I don't have enough experience.

I could go after that goal, but what if I fail?

I need to be perfect before I start.

Limiting beliefs are more deceptive than limited beliefs because they disguise themselves as logic. They don't outright tell you that success is impossible—they tell you that success is possible . . . just not for you. At least, not yet. These beliefs act as internal roadblocks, creating conditions, excuses, and fears that keep you from taking action.

Imagine someone who wants to start a YouTube channel but thinks, *I need to wait until I have the right equipment.* A month passes. Then a year. And before they know it, they've spent years "preparing" but never actually starting. That's the power of limiting beliefs—they create conditions that *feel* rational but ultimately keep you stuck.

Symptoms of Limiting Beliefs

- You want to take action but always find a reason to delay.
- You compare yourself to others and assume they have something you don't.
- You overthink every decision, afraid of making the "wrong" move.

3. Limitless Beliefs: The Mindset of Gurus

If they can do it, I can do it too.

I may not know how yet, but I'll figure it out.

Obstacles are just part of the process.

Limitless beliefs are what separate those who *talk* about success from those who actually achieve it. These are the beliefs of innovators, gurus, and visionaries. They don't see obstacles as stop signs; they see them as detours. They don't wait until they're "ready." They simply start and figure things out along the way.

A person with a limitless belief system doesn't look at a successful entrepreneur and think, *I could never do that.* Instead, they ask, *What can I learn from them? How can I apply that to my journey?* They see challenges not as proof that they're failing but as part of the inevitable path to success.

Signs of Limitless Beliefs

- You take action even when you don't feel 100% ready.
- You see failure as feedback, not a personal flaw.
- You believe success is *inevitable* as long as you keep moving forward.

FROM LIMITED TO LIMITLESS

In my experience, recognizing limiting beliefs (VOLT) is the first step. When you start questioning where these beliefs came from, you often realize they're not even yours—they're inherited.

If you've already been infected, don't worry—there's a way out. The world will always try to convince you that limitations are real, that success is reserved for a select few. But those who break free from VOLT redefine what's possible, refusing to accept the world as it is.

The key? Finding your own cure. There's no one-size-fits-all solution, because what works for one person may not work for another. Some people overcome VOLT through mentorship, others through therapy, spirituality, or deep self-reflection. The method doesn't matter—what matters is that you identify what strengthens your mindset and apply it every time self-doubt starts creeping in.

Surround yourself with the right people: mentors, coaches, or even friends who challenge you to think bigger. Read books that expand your perspective. Do the inner work. Every time you catch yourself hesitating, ask: *Whose limitations am I believing right now? And do they really belong to me?*

The shift from limited to limitless thinking takes time. Here's what I've seen work for others.

Step 1: Identify the Source

Every limitation you've internalized has an origin. Trace it back. Where did it start? Who planted that idea in your head? Was it a parent who doubted your abilities? A teacher who dismissed your talents? A friend who made a sarcastic remark that stuck with you?

Understanding the root cause of your limiting beliefs is the first step to breaking them.

Step 2: Reframe the Story

Once you identify the source, question it. Was this belief ever true? Or was it just someone else's fear passed onto you? Replace limiting beliefs with empowering alternatives:

- Instead of "Who am I to do this?" → **"Why *not* me?"**
- Instead of "What if I fail?" → **"What if I succeed?"**
- Instead of "I'm not as good as they think." → **"I bring something unique to the table."**

The only thing separating you from the most successful people in the world is their refusal to accept limitations. They aren't immune to doubt or VOLT, but they don't let it dictate their reality. Instead, they challenge it, push past it, and choose to define their own possibilities.

Step 3: Take Action Before You Feel Ready

VOLT thrives on inaction. The longer you wait to pursue your goals, the stronger it becomes. The antidote? Take action *before* you feel ready.

You don't need more time, more confidence, or more validation. You need momentum. Start before you feel qualified. Launch before you feel prepared. Confidence comes from doing, not waiting.

BREAKING FREE

Becoming a guru—whether in business, leadership, or as a thought leader—isn't about external validation. It's not about reaching a million followers, landing a TED Talk, or seeing your name in headlines. The real breakthrough happens when you break free from the limitations in your own mind.

I know this firsthand. For years, I believed that changing my environment would change me. I moved to new cities, launched new projects, reinvented myself over and over. But no matter how much I built on the outside, I carried the same unresolved doubts with me. I was running—chasing the idea that the *next* external success would finally make me feel like I had arrived. But here's the truth: Your external achievements will never outgrow your internal world. If you don't address the subconscious beliefs holding you back, they'll keep showing up—no matter how much money you make, how many people follow you, or how impressive your résumé becomes.

If you're aiming for high levels of success, the first step isn't about learning the latest strategy or chasing the next opportunity—it's about healing yourself. Because only when you clear the mental roadblocks standing in your way can you truly lead with confidence, clarity, and conviction.

Maybe you're not the exception you think you are. Maybe you belong in that advanced group and just need to claim your spot.

Chapter 15

THE GURU'S JOURNEY

Do not be embarrassed by your failures, learn from them and start again.

—Richard Branson

Throughout this book, we've explored the Guru Ladder, ROAC, positioning, and the external mechanics of building authority. But now we arrive at the heart of it all: the Guru's Journey—the internal transformation that makes everything else possible.

If you're anything like me, you've probably laid in bed wondering, *Will all this effort ever pay off?*

I first came across the "Six Phases of Mastery" while working at the Mike Ferry Organization. At the time, it was designed as a tool that described the journey of becoming a successful real estate agent. But later, I realized it described something much bigger: the emotional path every entrepreneurial expert walks while turning knowledge into influence.

It wasn't just about tactics. It reflected the real experience people go through in their business. The quiet stretches, self-doubt, small wins, and big setbacks. Over time, I stopped seeing it as theory and started using it as a map. And I've returned to it again and again, not because I stayed in real estate, but because the same cycle kept showing up as I built my brand and business or helped others build theirs.

I can't tell you how many times in my 15-year career I've cycled through these phases. By leveling up, only to hit a breakdown or setback. I've made mistakes not just once or twice, but over and over again. I've scrambled to get clients. I've lost everything and moved back into my parents' house at 30. I've felt stuck on a hamster wheel, doing the work but seeing no results. What helped me get through those moments wasn't just strategy, it was inner work. The more I shed limiting beliefs, the faster I could return to alignment, get back in motion, and climb again with clarity.

This is what I now call the Guru's Journey, the internal work that makes external growth possible. You may already know the Guru Ladder (Generalist → Specialist → Authority → Guru → Guru's Guru). That's the path of how your influence grows as others begin to see you differently. But this journey isn't just about climbing the ladder. It's about the internal shift that makes the climb real. It's the emotional process you go through that no one else sees. While your status may rise on the outside, this is about becoming the kind of person who feels aligned with the role you're stepping into.

You'll face resistance. Imposter syndrome. The fear of being seen too soon, or not seen at all. Especially in today's AI-driven world, it's tempting to think authority can be hacked or outsourced. But no amount of tech will replace the personal growth it takes to lead with trust and clarity. *Guru Inc.* is the result of aligning your identity, content, and business into one powerful system. It's not just about being visible. It's about being resonant. That's what the best personal brands do. They don't just perform, they transform.

BECOMING THE GURU

There's no clean formula for authority. It's not "post three times a week" or "build a funnel." The truth is: The Guru's Journey is messy. But it's also the most valuable transformation you'll ever go through.

You don't just learn strategies. You become someone who embodies them. Even as you rise from Specialist to Authority, or Authority to Guru, the challenges evolve. You'll face unfamiliar territory, need new systems, and circle back to old fears. But when you understand the six phases, the chaos feels less personal. You start to see each phase as a signal, not a setback. And that's the shift. The people we call "gurus" aren't perfect. They're just the ones who learned how to keep going. They know that breakdowns lead to breakthroughs. They've learned how to struggle well, and now they can lead others through it too.

Wherever you are on the ladder, this journey will meet you there, and help you move forward, stronger and more aligned than before.

PHASE 1: FORMULATION—GETTING CLEAR ON YOUR VISION

Formulation is the starting point of the Guru's Journey. This is where you begin building the foundation of your Personal Media Company. It's not just about launching a brand, it's about creating a channel people tune into because they associate you with a specific transformation. In this phase, you define what kind of show you're creating, who it's for, and what result it delivers. You don't need every detail figured out. What matters is clarity: the kind that lets you move forward with intention about the authority you want to become and the audience you're here to serve.

You'll activate the Three Strategic Moves:

1. **Own your category.** Choose your lane and position yourself as the obvious choice. Study your space. Where are the gaps or white space where you see an opportunity? What's being ignored? You're not here to be everything to everyone, you're here to be essential to certain groups.

2. **Create your method.** People want more than advice. They want a clear path. Your method is the framework that gets them results. It doesn't have to be perfect, just usable and repeatable. Ask yourself: What am I doing with clients or customers that consistently leads to their desired outcome? Whether it's through physical products, services, or content, your method should turn your expertise into a system others can trust.

3. **Build your programming.** Decide how your expertise will consistently show up online. Will you use short-form videos? Long-form vlogs? Personal stories? Your social-first show becomes the core structure for your channel.

Where you are on the Guru Ladder shapes how this looks:

Generalists define their specialty.

Specialists refine their positioning.

Authorities reframe their expertise with a media-first lens.

Behind the scenes, this phase is about structure. You'll research your audience. Not just demographics, but what keeps them up at night. Then define your content pillars, the core themes that anchor your brand. From there, choose your platform. You don't need to be everywhere. Just be consistent where it matters most.

This is also where resistance shows up. The moment you commit to a vision, VOLT (the Virus of Limited Thinking) creeps in. Doubts, perfectionism, imposter syndrome all flare up. *Who am I to do this? What if it's not good enough?* These are the blocks that stall creators at the bottom of the ladder. They stay stuck perfecting their website instead of publishing content that actually helps people. But the truth? Your audience doesn't care if your brand is flawless. They care if your message resonates and your content solves real problems.

Formulation isn't about perfection, it's about movement. Without clarity, your content will feel scattered. But with it, you gain the momentum needed for Phase 2: Concentration, where your ideas meet consistent execution.

Start by asking: What change do I want to create? Once you know that, the rest falls into place. Who do you need to be known as to make that change happen? What will you need to share, learn, and repeat to build that identity? When you can answer those questions, you're ready to move forward, even if it still feels a little messy. Because Formulation is about building with intention, not waiting for certainty.

PHASE 2: CONCENTRATION—WHERE THE REAL WORK BEGINS

If Formulation is about defining your vision, Concentration is where that vision starts to take shape. This is the phase where your Personal Media Company becomes real through consistent action. You're not just posting to stay busy, you're testing your positioning, message, and content structure in public.

Here, you apply your Three Strategic Moves. You reinforce your category by staying focused on your core themes. You refine your method by noticing what resonates. And you develop your programming by creating repeatable content formats your audience can recognize and return to: your social-first show.

What this looks like depends on your place on the Guru Ladder. Generalists and Specialists may lean into documenting: behind-the-scenes content, learning moments, or live problem-solving. Authorities might shift toward teaching: frameworks, insights, or bold takes. The key is sharing from where you are, not where you think you should be, and doing it consistently.

You're also testing different show formats. Maybe it's explainer-style videos in your car. Maybe it's playing two characters, walking through frameworks, or hosting mini-interviews at a conference. You're experimenting with hooks. You're intentionally creating curiosity gaps, pattern interruptions, or contrarian statements that stop the scroll and spark discussion.

You're not just watching views. You're paying attention to feedback. Are people commenting? Asking follow-ups? Sharing it with context? These signals, along with metrics, inform your ROAC (Return on Attention Created), helping you measure not just reach, but resonance.

You also start promoting content outside the platforms. Sharing videos with clients. Referencing posts in conversations. Linking great content in email newsletters or proposals. This isn't an ego thing, it's strategic self-promotion. You're creating touchpoints that allow your message to spread through relationships, not just algorithms.

But the real work here is rhythm. You publish consistently. You watch what works. You adapt. You develop stronger communication instincts and start shaping your message into a brand voice. You might not see explosive growth yet, but credibility is compounding behind the scenes.

That's why Concentration is hard. It's the grind before the break-through. The content creator's hamster wheel. You show up for weeks, sometimes months, and the numbers barely budge. It feels like you're doing everything right but getting no return. Most people quit here, not because they're wrong, but because they underestimate how long it takes for trust to build and systems to kick in.

But in the background, real progress is happening. The algorithm is learning who your audience is. Your network starts associating you with specific ideas. Clients begin repeating your language. Your ideas are gaining shape and traction, even if it's not fully visible yet.

One common trap in this phase is overstretching. You try to be on every platform. You start chasing every opportunity. But that's a recipe for burnout. Instead, focus on testing a few formats with intention, like pilots in a TV network. You don't need to go wide. You need to go deep. This is less about performance and more about identity. You're becoming the kind of person who shows up no matter what. That's the real win. That's how you build authority—before the audience arrives.

You'll know you're moving forward when your content rhythm feels manageable, engagement becomes more consistent, and you start seeing early signs of traction like comments, shares, or referrals. It begins to feel less like pressure and more like a habit. This usually takes about 90 days of consistent effort before you unlock real momentum. The Concentration phase is about trusting the process without applause. Every authority you admire has been through it. What sets them apart isn't talent. It's that they kept going when no one was watching.

PHASE 3: MOMENTUM—WHEN THINGS START ROLLING

After months of steady effort in Concentration, things begin to shift. You're becoming a sharper content creator and show developer. The formats you tested earlier are evolving into something more refined. You start to see what resonates. You'll understand what kind of hooks hold attention, which structures engage viewers, and which topics spark real conversations. Your content begins to feel less like random posts and more like a show people return to. Guesswork fades, and your consistency starts paying off.

Your positioning is clicking. Your audience begins to recognize your voice and anticipate your content. Inquiries become more frequent.

Clients, customers, or at least inquiries trickle in. People reference your ideas at events or mention they've been following you quietly for months. You're seeing more indirect value too. People are sending you referrals, word-of-mouth, and you see others applying your advice. Your ROAC becomes more visible through these real-world signals. You're moving from someone they follow to someone they rely on.

This phase can often last 6–18 months as you look to embrace the growth and stabilize. The challenge isn't overwhelming success; rather, it's staying consistent when growth feels slow but steady. Momentum is validating, but it brings new pressure. As opportunities increase, structure becomes essential. Without it, you may shift from leading to reacting. The same consistency that got you here now feels harder to maintain.

Ego and doubt also show up. You might believe you've figured it out and stop using the systems that built your success. Or old thoughts resurface, like *What if this doesn't last?* or *What if I'm not ready?* That tension can lead to self-sabotage just as traction begins.

To move through this phase well, observe and refine. Look closely at what content drives results. Identify which formats actually lead to valuable engagement or conversions, not just random views. Don't default to doing more. Do less, better. Say no more often. Deepen what's working instead of expanding in all directions.

You'll know you're progressing when growth feels predictable and sustainable. Opportunities begin to find you. You build small systems to maintain consistency without burnout. You prioritize long-term value over short-term noise. You start choosing from a place of clarity instead of urgency.

Momentum is not the finish line, it's the window. It asks whether you'll build something that lasts or get distracted by the next shiny thing. The people who make it through this phase are the ones who protect their energy, keep their rhythm, and stay anchored to their purpose.

The real test is continuing the structure and systems that got you here. You'll know you're moving through Momentum when your content process feels more fluid, your skills are sharper, and your belief in consistency is stronger than your need for instant results. Momentum isn't about going viral overnight. It's about recognizing that your foundation is starting to compound, and trusting that if you keep going, the rewards will scale with it.

PHASE 4: STABILIZATION—BUILDING YOUR EMPIRE

After months of steady momentum, a new challenge emerges: How do you keep growing without losing what made you successful in the first place?

This is where the Rubik's Cube analogy kicks in. You've solved the first two layers, but now every move affects everything else. Tweak your content, and it affects your offers. Adjust your business model, and it changes what kind of content you can sustain. Everything is connected, and without structure, one wrong move can scramble it all.

The solution is to stop winging it and start systematizing. You move from throwing things at the wall to executing with intent. In the show development phase we talked about in the previous chapter, we use a simple mix. Most of your content should focus on what already works. Utilize your strongest hooks and best-performing topics, and create from your winning show formats. A smaller portion should be dedicated to making small tweaks and optimizations. And a small slice should be your creative playground, where you test new concepts, formats, or bold swings. This structure keeps your content consistent without killing innovation.

What most people miss is that your content is no longer just content, it's fuel for your business engine. A great client result becomes a case study. That case study turns into content. That content draws in leads, which turn into more clients and more success stories. Your ROAC evolves from post-by-post wins to a flywheel that feeds itself. This results in your business becoming more demanding. More clients mean you need better delivery systems. More content means production, editing, and distribution can't rely on you alone. This is the stage where most entrepreneurial content creators realize they can't do everything themselves. You start building a team. Maybe it begins with a virtual assistant to help with project management, then an editor, and eventually a content manager. You're transitioning from solo creator to team leader.

And here's the part nobody warns you about: Success gets boring. When things run smoothly, the excitement of early growth wears off. You start thinking about switching platforms or reinventing your brand. I call this repetitious boredom, and it's more dangerous than an algorithm change. It convinces people to break what's working out of restlessness.

Instead of blowing things up, expand with intention. Launch spin-offs, adapt your format for new platforms, and build offers around what already works. Content brings people in, commerce turns trust into revenue, and concert makes it all flow together. When these align, growth compounds. You're not just making content anymore, you're running a media company built to scale.

PHASE 5: BREAKTHROUGH—WHEN GROWTH BECOMES EXPONENTIAL

After months or even years of steady work, a moment comes when everything suddenly accelerates. Breakthrough isn't gradual, it hits in bursts. Traffic spikes. Inquiries flood in. New opportunities appear out of nowhere. Your name shows up in rooms you've never entered. The uphill grind gives way to sudden momentum. This isn't just growth, it's transformation. It signals a shift in how the world sees you, and often marks your next move up the Guru Ladder.

What that breakthrough looks like depends on where you're starting. A Generalist might become known for a specific expertise. A Specialist could land a big client, book deal, or major speaking gig. For an Authority, this phase might launch them into full Guru status, where others start seeking your endorsement, perspective, or leadership. No matter your level, this stage changes how people engage with your work. It starts to feel bigger than you.

But external acceleration brings internal pressure. The speed can feel disorienting. Your team needs clear communication. Your systems need reinforcement. Your audience expects more from you, often before you've had time to recalibrate. What worked before may start to strain under the weight of new visibility, clients, and demands. You're no longer just creating content, you're managing perception, partnerships, and performance at scale.

Breakthrough often follows breakdown. The moment right before things pop is usually messy. Maybe you lost a client, hit burnout, or had something fall apart. But that low point sparked clarity. You faced the truth, shifted your approach, and showed up more aligned. That energy—raw and real—is often what cuts through and connects. Growth at this level rarely comes from playing it safe. It comes from evolution.

Breakthrough requires more stability, not less. You'll need better systems, clearer roles, and stronger boundaries. You'll revisit the rhythms that got you here. From content calendars and internal check-ins to delegation workflows—all of these will require a higher standard. What once worked casually now needs structure.

Some content creators rise again and again, each breakthrough elevating their influence. Others fall back if they don't adjust to the new level's demands. The key is understanding that breakthrough isn't a finish line, it's an invitation. It asks you to grow in leadership, mindset, and identity.

Breakthrough doesn't change who you are. It reveals who you've become. And what you do next determines how long you stay there.

PHASE 6: MASTERY—THE ULTIMATE DESTINATION

Mastery is the final phase of the Guru's Journey, and it's more attainable than ever. What once took decades can now happen in 3–10 years, thanks to AI and digital acceleration. That's why so many are drawn to personal brands. Reaching Guru or even Guru's Guru status—where your business runs on your Name, Image, and Likeness—is no longer a dream. It's a strategy.

At this stage, your Personal Media Company is no longer a solo operation. It's a full ecosystem. You have multiple shows across platforms, a flagship format, spin-offs, evergreen content libraries, and a powerful email engine. Your brand is omnipresent. Your audience doesn't just follow you, they live inside your brand world. They subscribe, share, attend, buy, and anticipate what's next.

You've built systems so solid, the business runs with or without you. Content, community, and commerce operate in sync. Excellence becomes your norm. You don't have to hustle daily for things to grow, your team, your brand assets, and your strategy do the work. This is true leverage.

At this level, you're not just known for your ideas, you're shaping your entire industry. Your frameworks become reference points. Your shows drive conversations far beyond your own audience. The Three Strategic Moves you built early on are now part of your team's DNA. The people executing them may even be better at their roles than you were.

That's not a threat to your leadership, it's a sign of it. Your content team helps you run shows that outperform your originals. Strategists spot opportunities you might miss. Community managers cultivate connection with care and precision. You've built not just a brand, but a legacy system others can operate and scale. So now opportunities come to you—like clients, partners, speaking invites, and media features—because your name precedes you. You can choose when to lean in or step back, because your influence grows even when your visibility doesn't.

Now, the game shifts again. You're playing at the guru level and the stakes feel lighter, not heavier. You have the freedom to choose what drives you. Maybe it's closing massive deals. Maybe it's mentoring rising authorities and seeing your methods change their lives. You're still ambitious, but from a place of grounded power. Many people in this phase also begin teaching others, not just for impact, but because helping others rise extends your reach. When those you mentor succeed, it confirms your role as a true leader. You're still evolving, still testing ideas, but now at scale, with more clarity and control.

Letting go of control becomes the final challenge. Many stall here because they're afraid quality will slip or their vision will dilute. But real Mastery means trusting what you've built: the systems, the people, the culture. You don't just manage a brand, you lead a movement.

You'll know you've reached Mastery when your frameworks and ideas are being taught by others, your peers study your playbook, and your impact grows even when you're hands-off. You're not just successful, but you've become the model others follow. Mastery isn't the end. It's the point where your work transcends you, and continues to shape the world long after you've stepped away.

KEY PITFALLS TO ADDRESS

The Guru's Journey isn't smooth. Setbacks are part of the path. What separates those who rise is how they respond. They catch issues early and return to what works.

There are two main setbacks to watch for: breakdowns and disasters.

Breakdowns

Breakdowns set you back a phase. They happen when you stop doing the basics like posting consistently, following your systems, staying in touch with your audience. Often, they creep in just as things start working. You feel momentum, then start skipping steps, thinking the results will sustain themselves. But slowly, your structure unravels.

This doesn't feel like failure at first. You're "just busy." You tell yourself it's temporary. But over time, you drift from your content plan, delay tough conversations, and react instead of lead. Your ROAC drops, not just in views, but in trust.

The root is often VOLT—the Virus of Limited Thinking. You start believing success isn't sustainable, or that you don't deserve it. You chase shortcuts or shiny tools. Ego can even tell you the basics no longer apply. The warning signs are subtle: Your work feels heavy, you improvise instead of execute, you chase opportunities that don't align. These are clues that you've veered off course.

The solution isn't to hustle harder. It's to return to your foundation. Recommit to the habits and systems that built your authority. Revisit your Three Strategic Moves. Talk to someone who can reflect the truth back to you, like a team member, a coach, a peer. Most importantly, look at what triggered the slide. Was it burnout? Comparison? Fear of success? Breakdowns are often the setup for breakthroughs—if you meet them with awareness and take action before they snowball.

Disasters

Disasters happen when breakdowns go unchecked. They don't just slow you down, they send you crashing back multiple phases. You abandon your systems. Your show goes dark. Your audience forgets. Your ROAC evaporates. It starts with silence. You stop posting. Emails go unanswered. Your presence fades, and with it, your momentum. What was once a thriving brand becomes a ghost town.

Disasters are usually driven by deeper issues: scaling too fast without support, losing sight of your strategy, or letting VOLT convince you your success was a fluke. Sometimes, you stretch yourself thin chasing ego-driven wins. Other times, you simply burn out and disappear. The effects run deep. Your audience disengages. Team members leave. Revenue dips. But the hardest part is internal: You lose confidence in your ability to lead. The identity you worked so hard to build starts to feel fake. The title you earned, Specialist, Authority, even Guru, feels distant.

The longer you stay in a disaster phase, the harder it is to return. But not impossible. You may have to drop back a few rungs, rebuild your structure, and regain trust. That takes work, but it's far easier to prevent disasters by recognizing early signs: long silences, stalled systems, lost clarity, and disconnection from your purpose.

Authority isn't permanent. It's a practice. When you stop honoring the habits that built your influence, that influence fades. But when you realign and recommit, you can return stronger. You'll be clearer, more grounded, and more resilient than before. The most important thing is this: Keep showing up—especially when it feels hard. That's what separates gurus who fade from those who rise again.

THE JOURNEY IS THE DESTINATION

This path isn't something you master once and leave behind. It loops back, asking more of you each time. That's not a flaw in the process—it *is* the process. Each phase doesn't just help you build your brand or business. It asks you to grow into a version of yourself you haven't met yet.

There will be seasons when you're creating in the dark, testing ideas and wondering if anyone is really listening. You'll battle VOLT telling you you're not ready or not enough. Then momentum hits. Your content starts converting. ROAC is working. But attention brings pressure, and new success demands new leadership.

Eventually, you find a rhythm. Your Three Strategic Moves become instinct. Systems click. Your message lands. Your Personal Media Company matures into real programming. But even then, something will shift. Whether a platform change, a market twist, or a breakthrough on the Guru Ladder, you'll face new doubts and new decisions.

This isn't failure. It's the cycle. Every new level revisits old lessons. Specialists becoming Authorities face identity friction. Gurus expanding into new markets drop back into Concentration. The Joshua Bell effect reminds you: Context shapes value regardless of how talented you are, and sometimes you must reinvent the way your audience experiences your work.

The people you admire haven't figured it all out. They've just learned to walk through the phases without resisting them. They know how to turn attention into impact, and how to serve without selling out. They've mastered the art of staying rooted while adapting fast.

There is no final arrival. But there is a version of you that grows more grounded every time you return to the work. You learn to see breakdowns as breakthroughs in disguise. You realize your content isn't just output, it's your programming, your proof of value, your system of trust. So wherever you are—Formulation, Concentration, Momentum, Stabilization, Breakthrough, or Mastery—you're not behind. You're right where you need to be. Keep building your brand. Keep serving. Keep becoming. The journey is doing its job. Let it.

Chapter 16

"DARKETING"

If once you start down the dark path, forever will it dominate your destiny.

—Yoda

Power messes with your head, and this is where the Guru's Journey gets dangerous. Most experts start with good intentions. They want to help people and build something great. But somewhere along the way, a few get swept up in their destructive tendencies of the ego. When this happens, they fall into a dangerous trap.

Instead of actually helping people, they start playing mind games. They exploit insecurities and fake trust to get what they want. Instead of serving their audience, they want their audience to serve them. In gaming terms, this is when players start using codes instead of developing real skill. This is where the shift to the dark side happens.

(You can do your best Darth Vader impersonation here.)

You may be wondering: *Why write about fake gurus and manipulation in a book about becoming a guru?* Because a true leader must understand what they stand against, as much as what they stand for.

The truth is, fame and influence can go either way. You can use them to actually help people, or you can use them to manipulate people for your own benefit. Many gurus start with good intentions, only to be consumed by the very power they sought.

FROM SELFLESS TO SELFISH

The shift happens quietly when the allure of more takes hold. More followers. More money. More influence. And suddenly, the audience isn't a community anymore—it's a resource to be mined.

At first, it's just a little exaggeration, a hint of fake scarcity, a carefully staged success story. But these small distortions snowball, turning influence into manipulation, and authority into control. What starts as a personal brand evolves into an empire built on false promises, manufactured credibility, and fear-based persuasion.

And that's why so many gurus take the easier path, the "darketing" path: manipulating attention rather than building genuine influence. Because in a world where attention is currency, it's often faster to exploit emotions than to earn trust. Faster to manufacture authority than to build it. Faster to sell a dream than to teach a skill. Darketing isn't just about lying—it's about warping reality to create demand, trust, and dependency without delivering real substance. The goal isn't to solve problems but to keep people trapped in an endless cycle of needing more.

But shortcuts have consequences. Darketing is an ethical failure, but it's also a strategy with an expiration date. The moment people realize they've been played, trust erodes, reputations crumble, and the empire built on deception comes crashing down.

THE FIVE CORE TACTICS OF DARKETING

With the rise of social media short-form vertical video on TikTok, Instagram Reels, and YouTube Shorts, nearly anyone can go viral or amass significant viewership rather quickly. The barriers to entry have never been lower, and algorithms don't have a moral compass—they simply reward engagement. This means bad actors slip through the cracks, and fake gurus who lack real experience, wisdom, or skill can manufacture credibility overnight. Instead of delivering real value, they rely on gimmicky manipulation tactics—staging fake interviews, buying followers, and using black-hat marketing techniques to fabricate success.

But as an expert creating content, it's crucial to find your true north. This isn't about playing it safe, avoiding strong opinions, or refusing to sell. You can be bold and still make serious money without compromising your integrity. The real issue isn't about being edgy—it's about crossing the line where you start taking advantage of your audience.

To avoid falling into the same trap as so many others, you need to recognize where things go wrong. Not everything designed to capture attention is inherently unethical or deceptive. A strong hook, scarcity-driven offers, and emotional storytelling can all be powerful tools when used with integrity. The problem starts when these tactics are used to exploit rather than engage—when persuasion shifts into manipulation.

This is where darketing thrives: in that gray area where strategies that could educate and empower are twisted to mislead and exploit.

To help you steer clear of this path, you need to recognize the five core tactics of darketing that fake gurus use to cheat the system. These are the red flags that separate ethical influence from manipulation—and understanding them will help you avoid falling into the trap yourself.

1. Dark User Experience (UX) Patterns: When Design Becomes Deception

Have you ever tried canceling a subscription and felt like you were being led in circles? That's not an accident, it's by design. Have you ever signed up for a "free trial," only to realize later that you were unknowingly locked into a paid plan? Also by design.

Dark UX patterns use deceptive design to manipulate user behavior—making it harder to opt out, obscuring costs, or tricking people into actions they didn't intend. These tactics don't just frustrate users, they exploit them.

Some of the biggest companies in the world have been called out for these practices. Take, for example, Amazon's "Iliad flow," which is where Amazon deliberately made canceling Prime so convoluted that users would give up before completing the process. The Federal Trade Commission eventually sued Amazon for these tactics, proving that deception has real consequences.

Even LinkedIn, the corporate social media behemoth, is guilty of confusing UX aimed at trapping its subscribers. LinkedIn once tricked users into unknowingly sending invitations to their entire contact list, making it seem like a normal feature. The result? Millions of people unintentionally spamming their friends and colleagues. These examples teach us the importance of being transparent about terms, pricing, and conditions, and eliminating the need for hidden tricks. If you want to keep your audience loyal, committed, and engaged, you'll want to make your brand ecosystem as easy to *leave* as it is to *join*. If it's hard for users to leave your ecosystem, you're prioritizing profit over trust.

2. Algorithmic Manipulation: Overpromising & Underdelivering

The internet doesn't always reward truth—it rewards whatever gets the most clicks. In the world of darketing, that means sensational claims, exaggerated promises, and content designed to grab attention without actually delivering value. Algorithms don't care about integrity; they prioritize engagement, allowing misleading tactics to thrive.

A common example is the flood of online ads claiming, "I made $10K in a week, and you can too!" On the surface, it sounds like an exciting opportunity. But dig deeper, and the entire system is often nothing more than a cycle of selling courses on how to sell courses. There's no real skill, no proven system—just an endless loop of manufactured success, where the only ones truly making money are those selling the illusion.

Another deceptive strategy is the so-called secret method that promises to reveal a groundbreaking strategy, only to deliver vague fluff and empty hype. Instead of real insights, the creator dangles just enough intrigue to keep viewers hooked, while the only real secret is how much money they're making off the bait and switch.

This is why integrity matters. If you're going to make a bold claim, back it up. Deliver on what you promise, instead of relying on hype as a substitute for substance. Avoid the trap of mystery-box marketing, where people are strung along by endless curiosity with little to no value in return. Real trust is built through transparency and follow-through, not deception wrapped in clever packaging.

3. Fake Authority: The Illusion of Success

Not all gurus are self-made. Some are self-fabricated. Instead of building credibility through real expertise and results, they manufacture the appearance of success. In the digital world, perception is reality, and those who understand this can craft an illusion of authority without ever proving their worth.

A common tactic is the carefully curated lifestyle of so-called business coaches flaunting luxury cars and private jets. What many don't realize is that these images are often staged—exotic cars are rented for the day, and photoshoots in front of private jets are nothing more than props in a marketing strategy. The goal isn't to showcase real success but to manufacture the appearance of wealth, knowing that people are more likely to trust those who seem to have already "made it."

True authority isn't built on rented status symbols or manipulated credentials; it comes from experience, results, and a real track record. The key to lasting influence isn't in crafting an illusion but in providing substance. A well-curated image may capture attention, but only real value and authenticity will hold it.

4. Manipulative Psychological Triggers: Fear, FOMO & Forced Action

The easiest way to get people to act is by making them afraid of missing out. When faced with the possibility of regret, people make impulsive decisions, often against their better judgment. Darketing thrives on this vulnerability, using artificial scarcity and fear-based messaging to push people into taking action before they have time to think.

Some of the most common tactics involve creating a false sense of urgency. A countdown timer on a sales page may suggest an offer is about to disappear, yet refreshing the page magically resets the clock. Limited-time deals may not be limited at all but instead part of an endless sales cycle designed to pressure customers into buying immediately.

Another variation of this tactic plays on the illusion of exclusivity. Prerecorded webinars, for example, can be a great tool for education and sales, but when they are framed as live without disclosure, they become misleading. Some marketers set up automated webinars that simulate real-time engagement, pretending to respond to "live" comments or acting as if attendees are part of a one-time-only event when, in reality, the session is running on an endless loop. Instead of simply offering on-demand content, they create an artificial sense of urgency, leading viewers to believe they'll miss out on something unique if they don't act now.

Real urgency should be based on legitimate factors, like limited inventory or live event capacity, rather than fabricated pressure. Trust is built when audiences feel empowered to make decisions—not when they're forced into them.

But AJ, digital products have no inventory. How do I create real urgency without faking it?

The key is to create scarcity in a genuine and value-driven, rather than arbitrary, way. Digital products may be infinitely replicable, but certain elements, like direct access, coaching, pricing tiers, or exclusive bonuses, are naturally limited. For example, cohort-based enrollment means that access is only available at certain times to ensure students receive full support. Time-limited bonuses, like exclusive Q&A sessions or private coaching, make acting now more rewarding without being deceptive. Price increases over time also create an organic reason (unlike using false deadlines, for example) to buy early. Instead of making people feel pressured, real scarcity should be framed as an opportunity, where they aren't being forced to act but are rewarded for acting now.

5. Addiction & Engineered Dissatisfaction: The Cycle of Never-Ending Need

Great marketing solves problems. Darketing, on the other hand, ensures problems never feel fully solved. Instead of helping people move forward, it keeps them in a loop—always feeling like they're one step away from real success, happiness, or self-improvement. The goal isn't to create satisfied customers; it's to create dependent ones.

This strategy thrives in industries that profit from insecurity. The beauty industry, for example, is constantly inventing new "flaws" to fix—tech neck, hip dips, forehead wrinkles at 20. Each new term plants the idea that something is wrong, reinforcing the belief that perfection is always just out of reach. No matter how much someone invests in their appearance, there's always a new issue to address, a new product to buy, and a new standard to chase.

The self-help industry plays a similar game. Instead of empowering transformation, some programs are structured to keep people in an endless cycle of self-work. There's always another level, another mindset shift, another course that promises to unlock what they've been missing. Growth is dangled like a finish line that keeps moving, keeping customers hooked rather than truly independent.

Tech companies also walk this fine line. Many brands, like Apple, offer genuine innovation, with each new device bringing real advancements in speed, design, or functionality. But at the same time, engineered dissatisfaction plays a role in driving upgrades. Some tactics, like limiting software support for older models or marketing minor improvements as game changers, create a psychological need to upgrade even when the product someone already owns works just fine. The strategy isn't about deceiving customers outright, it's about shaping their perception of what they "need."

Social media accelerates all this, fueling a sense of comparison and inadequacy. Instead of measuring progress against their own journey, people are constantly exposed to curated highlight reels of success, beauty, and achievement. The result? A nagging feeling that they're never doing enough, never earning enough, never improving fast enough, so they keep searching for the next big solution.

The real problem isn't wanting more, it's the belief that you're never enough without it. Ethical marketing provides real solutions that empower people to move forward. If you're creating something valuable, your audience should return because they trust you, not because they feel trapped in an endless cycle of dissatisfaction.

THE RISE AND FALL OF FAKE GURUS

Darketing isn't just a theory, it plays out in real life. Fake gurus are real, and you've probably even heard some of their names. They've mastered the art of manufacturing trust, using hype and deception to create an illusion of success.

But as history has shown, darketing only works until it doesn't. When the truth comes out, the empire they built on manipulation collapses, often spectacularly, taking their reputation, fortune, and followers with it.

Here are some of the most infamous cases where darketing led to downfall. These stories aren't just scandals; they're cautionary tales of what happens when influence is built on deception instead of real impact.

Bikram Choudhury: The Cult of Personality

Bikram Choudhury built a yoga empire by positioning himself as the sole authority on the Bikram method. His leadership didn't just attract followers, it demanded them. Strict rules, psychological manipulation, and unchecked power created an environment where questioning him was seen as betrayal. What started as a movement for wellness became a system of control.

For years, his carefully cultivated image of a devoted guru remained intact. But as allegations of sexual misconduct, verbal abuse, and financial exploitation surfaced, the foundation of his influence crumbled. His power wasn't built on trust, it was built on obedience. And when that obedience was no longer absolute, his downfall was certain.

True influence isn't about making people dependent on you, it's about making them stronger. If success hinges on blind loyalty rather than real value, the brand is just waiting to collapse.

Belle Gibson: The Cancer Con

Belle Gibson built an empire on a lie. She rose to fame as a wellness influencer, claiming she had cured her terminal brain cancer through natural remedies, clean eating, and holistic health practices, all while promoting a best-selling book and a widely popular wellness app. Her story was powerful, inspiring thousands to adopt her lifestyle and buy into her brand. But there was one problem: She never had cancer.

For years, Gibson manipulated her audience, fabricating symptoms and survival stories, and even promising to donate portions of her earnings to charity—which never happened. When journalists began questioning inconsistencies in her timeline, the truth unraveled, and the backlash was swift. Her book was pulled from shelves, her app was shut down, and she was eventually fined for misleading consumers.

Gibson's downfall was a brutal reminder that fabricated authority, especially in health and wellness, is not just unethical, it's dangerous. When people trust you with their health, their money, or their future, they're placing real stakes in your guidance. And when that trust is built on deception, the collapse is inevitable.

Sam Bankman-Fried: The Crypto Illusion

Once hailed as the golden boy of cryptocurrency, Sam Bankman-Fried built his reputation as an altruistic billionaire, a financial revolutionary who claimed to be reshaping the industry for the better. But behind the carefully curated narrative, his company, FTX, was built on deception, manipulating investors, misusing customer funds, and projecting an illusion of stability that never existed.

When the truth came out, his empire collapsed overnight. The fallout wasn't just financial; it sent shockwaves through an already volatile crypto industry, eroding trust and leaving thousands of investors with billions in losses. The lesson was clear: Hype without substance is a ticking time bomb.

Success built on illusion never lasts. The strongest brands, whether in finance, business, or content creation, are the ones that don't just capture attention but sustain it with real value. If the foundation of a business relies on secrecy and deception, its collapse is only a matter of time.

Elizabeth Holmes: The Silicon Valley Scam

Elizabeth Holmes didn't just sell a product—she sold a persona. Modeled after Steve Jobs, complete with the signature black turtleneck, she positioned herself as a visionary set to revolutionize healthcare. Her company, Theranos, promised a groundbreaking blood-testing device that could diagnose diseases with just a few drops of blood. Investors, media outlets, and even world leaders bought into the vision without questioning a simple but critical detail: Did the technology actually work?

It didn't. Theranos was built on false claims, faked test results, and a carefully managed media presence that reinforced Holmes as the next great innovator. The illusion held for years, sustained by high-profile endorsements and a culture of secrecy. But when whistleblowers exposed the truth, the house of cards collapsed. Holmes wasn't just a failed entrepreneur, she was convicted of fraud.

Perception can open doors, but expertise keeps them open. Selling a dream is one thing, but when success depends on faking results to sustain the illusion, is it really success? True authority isn't about image, it's about delivering on what you promise.

Liver King: The Lie Behind the Lifestyle

Liver King built a multimillion-dollar brand on the promise of the "ancestral lifestyle," eating raw liver, rejecting modern medicine, and training like a primal warrior. His shredded physique was the proof, and his aggressive marketing turned his philosophy into a movement. He wasn't just selling supplements; he was selling an identity.

But the entire image was a fabrication. Leaked emails revealed that his caveman-like strength wasn't the result of organ meats and primal living, it was the result of thousands of dollars in steroids each month. The very foundation of his brand was built on a lie, and when the truth surfaced, trust in him collapsed overnight.

Authenticity isn't a marketing strategy, it's the foundation of lasting influence. If you build a brand around your personal journey, that journey needs to be real. The moment your audience discovers they've been misled, credibility is lost. And in the world of influence, credibility is everything.

Each of these cases shows what happens when you try to cheat the system. The game always catches up with exploiters eventually. Real gurus build lasting influence through skill, not shortcuts.

WHY DO PEOPLE FOLLOW FAKE GURUS?

For as long as humans have been able to communicate, we've had the ability to bend the truth: sometimes to inspire, sometimes to manipulate.

Fake gurus don't just sell a product or an idea; they sell certainty in an uncertain world. They offer shortcuts, claiming to have the formula for success. And for those struggling to navigate their own path, the promise of a guaranteed outcome is incredibly tempting.

The damage, however, extends beyond the individual. When a guru betrays trust, it doesn't just discredit them, it creates skepticism that ripples through entire industries. Once someone has been burned by false promises, they become wary of anyone offering a similar path, making it harder for legitimate voices to break through.

Think about it, if you had invested thousands into a program promising to transform your business, only to walk away with nothing but empty motivational fluff, would you be eager to trust the next expert who claims to be the one who is going to help you? Probably not.

This is why the rise of fake gurus has created an environment of distrust. They prey on people's deepest dreams: not just financial freedom but also health, happiness, love, and fulfillment, packaging success into one-size-fits-all courses that promise effortless paths to wealth, perfect bodies, ideal relationships, or lasting happiness.

The truth is, many people look to gurus hoping they'll deliver a single piece of wisdom that will fix everything, a secret method that will instantly remove obstacles, erase self-doubt, and hand them success on a silver platter. But no guru can do that.

WHAT YOU DO WHEN NO ONE'S WATCHING

In Hindu mythology, the god Brahma was cursed never to be worshiped, because he abused his power. Even in ancient wisdom, the lesson is clear: There are always consequences for deception. The same applies to modern influence. Attention is a currency, but what you do with it is what defines you.

Marketing isn't inherently manipulative. Selling isn't inherently deceptive. But the moment the goal shifts from serving people to exploiting them, that's where the damage begins. It's not about what you can get away with, it's about what happens when people realize the truth. And they always do.

And remember, your reputation isn't built on what you say about yourself—it's built on what others say when you're not in the room.

Chapter 17

THE POWER OF SELFLESSNESS

Serving Your Audience

The best way to find yourself is to lose yourself in the service of others.

—Mahatma Gandhi

Growing up, my family taught me the value of *seva*, which means "selfless service." We practiced it regularly at our local gurdwara, a house of worship that means "the door to the guru." My mother was Sikh and my father was Hindu, so our household blended different traditions, but *seva* was central to both.

At the gurdwara, people practice *seva* by volunteering as *sevadars*. These are basically the helpers who serve the community. But I learned that the *sevadar* concept is much bigger than just being a volunteer at a spiritual function. The principles of *sevadar* extend beyond the spiritual setting and apply to business as well.

I've found that service works best when it just becomes part of who you are. I remember as a child watching a very unusual experience. The adults would sometimes actually get into arguments over who got to serve that day—that's how passionate people were about being of service!

WHAT MOST PEOPLE DON'T KNOW ABOUT LOVE

When you set out on a journey of selfless service, you have to retrain your brain to recognize that love is much more than a romantic attraction. In my experience, love shows up more in actions than feelings. It's the daily work of caring for someone or something beyond yourself.

Think about your favorite soft and cuddly cat or dog. Just thinking of your pet can conjure all sorts of feelings of love. But what about when it's time to clean up their messes, or pay for their vet bills? What is more loving: petting your cat on the couch and listening to them purr, or taking them to the vet when they are suffering in pain? Sometimes, the loving action isn't easy, and other times, to serve the people you love, love requires doing things that really suck. Love is personified best when you use your time, talent, and treasure to serve others. At the end of the day, true service can only come from a place of love.

Let me give you a story that illustrates this concept of a purpose-driven approach perfectly.

The Story of the Janitor and the Astronaut

President John Fitzgerald Kennedy was young and ambitious. Wherever he went, people stood in rapt attention. Crowds flocked to see him, and thousands would stand in awe of his motorcade as it drove past. You could say he was a guru's guru. One of my favorite stories about him is when he went on a tour of NASA, the most impressive space agency in the world at that time.

On his tour, Kennedy noticed a man who was doing custodial work. He was nothing more than a humble janitor. But he was working incredibly hard to clean the floors. Why was this man working so hard?

Kennedy stopped and asked him what he was doing. He was curious. The man set his broom and mop down, looked up at the most powerful leader in the free world, and smiled. Kennedy repeated, "What is your role here, sir?"

The man didn't miss a beat. Beaming with pride, one hand on his mop, the other on the broom, he confidently looked up at Kennedy and said, "I'm helping put a man on the moon."

His answer took Kennedy by surprise. He was left speechless. This janitor's response stuck with me because it showed how someone could see their role differently. Instead of just cleaning floors, he saw himself as part of something bigger—the mission to put a man on the moon. You see, what the janitor knew is that every person in a company or organization has an important role to play to further the mission of the company. This man was not a trained astronaut. In the eyes of the public, he was in the lowliest position at NASA. But in his eyes, he was a vital part of serving a much larger mission. And that's the realization that love embodies: hard work, sacrifice, and service to others. Love knows that every person, no matter how insignificant the contribution may seem, is working toward that higher act of service.

For me, this story is love as a service personified, and it is one of my favorite teaching moments when I think about remaining humble and learning to serve my clients better. The guru doesn't ask, "How can I get something from this other person?" Instead, they constantly ask themselves, "How can I help?"

So where does this conversation connect to your aspirations to become a business guru?

YOU WANT TO CHANGE THE WORLD

If you're reading this book, there's a good chance you have expertise you want to share with the world. You've likely felt the satisfaction of helping someone solve a real problem. You're passionate about using your unique knowledge to make a difference, and you love seeing your insights truly resonate with others. Most of all, you want to reach a larger audience with the meaningful, heart-centered solutions you're here to offer.

For aspiring gurus, like you, who want to change the world, I have a solution for how you can have more of all three of these things in your life. And the best part is that it's a really simple solution that you can embody, starting today, with just a subtle mindset tweak.

Influencers focus on results, but gurus are masters at bringing out people's latent passions. They fire up the crowd with a renewed sense of purpose, excitement and energy. They do it by loving what they do. And they pass on this love to their followers. You've probably seen a singer onstage or a football star on the field get a crowd of 50,000 people excited. The energy is electrifying and contagious. When you are serving a bigger mission than yourself, it can literally help put a human on the moon!

When you create content, you may not be sitting in an arena of 50,000 people, but in reality, you have access to thousands more all over the globe! When you love what you do, and share that excitement with them, you are generating goodwill within your community. You work hard at creating all this content, then dish it up and serve it out to the masses for free. This is selfless service. The biggest thing that gurus have to understand is that it's not about you, it's about them, the audience.

But what often trips people up on their pathway toward serving others and becoming a guru is that their ego gets in the way. Instead of selflessly serving others, they become primarily self-serving. We saw an example of this in the darketing chapter. They think posting selfies with famous people and celebrities and talking about all their accomplishments is the pathway to success. Newsflash: This may work in the early stages, but it isn't sustainable to level up the Guru Ladder. It's like eating chocolate cake for breakfast, lunch, and dinner. It may give you a quick boost, but eventually, no matter how much you eat, it will lead to an even bigger crash.

When you focus on the lack of your guru-ness, you can get sucked into a scarcity mindset that makes you feel like you need to compete to be better than all the other gurus out there, instead of seeing the abundance of creative potential right in front of you that is available through service.

People are always telling me they need the "right opportunity" to get to where they want to be in their careers. But the truth is, the opportunity to serve and solve problems is available to you 24/7/365. The only thing you need to do is grab it.

Life is full of problems, complications, setbacks, and confusion, so the chances are extremely high that someone out there right now is scouring the internet looking for help with a problem that you could solve! Remember, love is an action. Taking action to help others is how you get to become a guru. When the guru takes the stage, they don't stand up there and brag about their accomplishments. They teach, they make themselves available, and they freely give their time and talent to solve other people's problems.

BEWARE OF ENTITLEMENT

In our social media world, money is the by-product of good service. I've noticed that some content creators expect immediate recognition for their expertise. They focus on getting followers and acclaim before proving their value. In my experience, the order matters—service first, recognition second.

The doorway to becoming the guru is all about serving first and getting recognition second. It's the popular "be-do-have" principle in action. This concept goes hand in hand with being a *sevadar*, although I'm pretty sure I may be the only person who thinks about it like that.

Be-do-have means: who you are being, what you are doing, and what you are having. And it's in that order for a reason: What you have is the by-product of the first two. But when most people start a business seeking to become a guru, they have it backward—they want to have acclaim and success first, and then they will do the hard work to get it.

For example, clients come to me all the time saying things like, "AJ, I want to have a successful company. Once I have investors who will give me the money, then I'll start working to build the company." Or, my personal favorite: "AJ, I want millions of followers, but I don't want to spend the time every day on social media to grow my following."

This is a very entitled approach. People complain about not getting millions of views on social media platforms, but what they forget is that they aren't grateful for the views they are already getting. They don't care about the hundreds or thousands of people they've helped in their careers. They want to be Tony Robbins or Oprah Winfrey and help millions of people. But this isn't true service. This is just another trick of the ego.

"I just want to help as many people as possible" is another common phrase I hear all the time. But is this really authentic? Is what they actually mean, "I just want to make as much money as possible?"

Wannabe gurus say they want to help, but they don't want to commit to the labor of actually scooping the soup into the bowl. They don't want to actually serve and exchange value in the form of labor. Instead, they just give these lofty ideals lip service, because they know it sounds good at a networking event or when they are prospecting for new potential clients.

A lot of people smarter than me have written things like, "It's the journey and not the destination," or, "Trust the process." But what I've found is a shortcut to tapping into this mindset. What I've found is that when you genuinely enjoy helping your community, everything else becomes easier. The content creation, the long hours, even the criticism—it all feels more manageable when you're focused on the impact you're making.

Building guru status requires consistent effort, even when the work isn't glamorous. There's a misconception that you only do what you love, but sometimes you're filing taxes or handling mundane tasks. When this happens, remember to be like the janitor who, despite not having a glamorous role at NASA, was remembered for not only helping to put a man on the moon but, more importantly, being excellent at his craft.

That type of intense dedication to work ethic is only possible when you truly love something. If you love it, you will be much more likely to chase after your dreams, even when it isn't easy or convenient for you. And when you love the work you do, and serve your community from a place of love, the people you serve will love you for it. I've found that the most sustainable influence comes from empowering others rather than controlling them. The alternative, manipulation for personal gain, tends to backfire eventually. It's what fake gurus do. It's what I've been calling darketing. When you lead from a place of true empowerment rather than ego-driven control, it has the power to create a ripple effect that creates more love in the world.

Adopting a service-first mindset is one of the fastest ways to quiet imposter syndrome. As business gurus like Tony Robbins love to say: "When you're focused on serving, you stop obsessing over yourself." I've seen it again and again, brilliant entrepreneurs who suddenly tense up when it's time to sell. They worry they're taking something from people, usually money. What I've noticed is that when you focus on serving, selling feels different. Instead of feeling like you're taking something, it feels like you're offering a solution. And that changes everything.

The concept of "serve, don't sell" is the foundation of impactful thought leadership and effective marketing. At its core, this principle shifts the focus from pushing products or self-promotion to genuinely understanding and addressing the needs of an audience. Gurus like

Oprah Winfrey, Ellen DeGeneres, and Martha Stewart didn't build their empires by selling aggressively; they built trust and loyalty by consistently serving their followers—whether through transformative conversations, uplifting entertainment, or practical tools for better living.

By prioritizing service, they created emotional connections that fostered long-term engagement and inspired change. This approach positions thought leaders and marketers as healers, offering solutions that not only solve surface-level problems but also address deeper, more meaningful challenges. In my experience, the "serve, don't sell" approach tends to build more sustainable influence than aggressive promotion tactics ever could.

Chapter 18

EMBRACING THE GURU WITHIN

Awakening the Power in You

Great leaders create more leaders, not followers.

—Roy T. Bennett

To become a guru, you have to get your own shit together first. Self-control and emotional clarity aren't optional, they're everything. When you do the inner work, when you confront your blind spots, rewire your beliefs, and move from fear to clarity, you don't just grow. You become someone others trust to follow. That's the secret most people miss: Thought leadership doesn't start with content. It starts with character.

Embracing the guru within means recognizing that the wisdom and authority you seek externally already exists inside you. This can be a difficult concept to grasp, but at the forefront of every successful guru is an incredible superpower: self-belief.

When you believe in yourself, you naturally exude confidence. This confidence is incredibly powerful because it acts as a magnet that attracts the best business opportunities to you. People look up to leaders who value themselves and know their self-worth. But sometimes highly talented creators can be riddled with self-doubt and fall victim to imposter syndrome because they feel like they have to be one of the top performers in their niche.

One of the common pitfalls that I see experts fall into on their climb up the Guru Ladder is that they try to be the best at what they do *before* they start promoting themselves. I want to provide you with a gentle reminder: *It's not about being the best at what you do—it's about being the best at getting the world to see it.*

It's the age-old question: If a tree falls in the forest and no one hears it, does it make a sound? If a creator posts on social media and no one sees it, does it make an impression? The takeaway I want you to remember is that expertise alone isn't enough; mastering attention is what separates obscurity from industry dominance.

In the war for attention, the market is flooded with content from brands, experts, and even AI, but only those who master positioning and visibility will stand out. Attention is the ultimate currency in today's economy. People don't buy the best product or service—they buy what they know exists. Look at who wins: Oprah, MrBeast, Neil Patel, and Gary Vee—they're not necessarily the best in their field, but they're the best at capturing attention and turning it into influence and wealth.

That said, before a guru can capture attention, they must first be worthy of it. True thought leadership isn't just about visibility; it's about having something worth seeing. That process is internal. Before leading others, a guru must first lead themself. Clarity of purpose, alignment with one's message, and confidence in one's expertise are what make a personal brand magnetic. The greatest gurus aren't chasing applause or external validation from their peers on social media; they architect their own narrative and let the right people find them. They understand that attention alone isn't the goal—attention is just a means to make more of an impact.

After all, not all attention is good attention. Some chase influence through controversy, deception, or playing the algorithm at all costs. But true gurus build sustainable influence dependent not on trends but on real, lasting authority.

Before you put this book down and go out to implement the action items you've learned, I want to give you a quick recap of some of the main themes we've explored here.

- **Master Context, Not Just Content:** Positioning and storytelling are what turn experts into gurus.

- **ROAC (Return on Attention Created):** It's not about vanity metrics, it's about real-world impact. The real game is converting attention into identity, trust, and leverage.

- **Own the Platform, Own the Market:** True gurus don't just participate in the conversation—they own the distribution (media companies, product lines, licensing deals).

- **Be Omnipresent or Be Forgotten:** Dominate the spaces where your audience lives across all channels. Don't settle for just being highly visible on one platform, or you will risk being forgotten. The market won't wait for you. If you don't master attention now, someone else will. The era of "letting your work speak for itself" is over—without strategic positioning, even the best ideas will die in obscurity.

As I reflect on this journey, I'm reminded that none of us climb the Guru Ladder alone. The relationships that shaped me early on have evolved in remarkable ways. Sanjay and I reconnected after our grandfather passed away, and it was inspiring to see him thriving in his calling—working with clients on mindset coaching, leading seminars, and speaking with that dynamic energy I'd always admired. Neil Patel has built NP Digital into one of the world's leading advertising agencies with over 1,000 employees, serving everyone from small businesses to enterprise clients. I'm grateful to still work with him, helping with his social media and personal brand while continuing to learn from the mentor who started it all. And Jason has been my business partner and co-owner in The Limitless Company. We've built it together into what it is today.

Both Neil and Sanjay filled the older brother role I'd always longed for as the oldest child in my family, showing me what was possible and pushing me to be better. But somewhere along this journey, I realized I'd been seeking externally what I could embody myself. I was already Jason's older brother, and I could be that same guiding presence for my clients and community. The cycle continues: We all need mentors to guide us, and we all have the responsibility to guide others. These relationships remind me that true guru status isn't just about individual achievement; it's about how we elevate each other along the way.

SOCIAL MEDIA IS JUST A MIRROR

Becoming a guru isn't about the world seeing you—it's about you seeing yourself, fully and unapologetically. True mastery begins with self-awareness. Social media is a powerful tool to show your work to others, but it is also a mirror that helps you see yourself clearly. A guru is defined not by their followers, accolades, or external validation but by their ability to embrace and embody their authentic self. It's a journey of peeling back the layers of societal conditioning, self-doubt, and fear to uncover the core of who you truly are. That's the real magic behind this book. Because when you fully see yourself—your strengths, weaknesses, passions, and purpose—you step into an undeniable power. That's my goal for you!

This process isn't about perfection, it's about acceptance. It's about being courageous enough to face your inner truths and resilient enough to align your life and your business mission with them. Becoming a guru means breaking free from the need to perform for others and instead leading from a place of integrity and conviction. The world's recognition is secondary to your own self-recognition. These can be hard truths, but they are important lessons that every guru must learn along their journey.

When you see yourself fully, you no longer chase external approval, because you've built an unshakable foundation within. You become a magnet for others not because of what you do but because of who you are. Your authenticity resonates, and that resonance is what creates real influence and impact.

In this way, the journey of becoming a guru is deeply personal before it is ever public. It's about healing the parts of you that have been hidden, integrating the parts of you that feel fragmented, and unapologetically owning the truth of your existence. Only then can you inspire others to do the same. The world seeing you is merely the reflection of you finally seeing yourself.

You don't win the new media game by being the best—you win by being impossible to ignore. You now have all the crucial pieces to win: the goals (Guru Ladder), the strategic moves (ROAC), how to overcome internal blocks (VOLT), and what the journey actually feels like (Six Phases of Mastery). The game doesn't end when you become a guru; that's just when you unlock the next level of impact and influence.

AFTERWORD
The Final Awakening

A large crowd of thousands of people sat attentively, their collective gaze—tens of thousands of eyeballs—fixed on the man I knew as my family's guru. If you asked him about KPIs or how he measured his ROAC, he likely couldn't answer. This wasn't Mike Ferry or Neil Patel. He looked softly at the woman holding the microphone. While her hand clutched the device, I could tell she was holding back tears.

Baba Ji sat on a chair in front of the crowd, creating space for her to share. She explained that her mother had recently passed away and asked if her soul would ever recognize her mother's soul again when she goes to heaven. The room fell silent as everyone awaited his response to this poignant moment.

It was a profound question and not something a marketer like myself can attempt to answer in this book. But Baba Ji's response changed my perspective on life and humanity that day. His beautifully lucid words tugged at everyone's heartstrings. Many women reached for tissues to save their makeup from tears. I'll share Baba Ji's quote shortly, but first, I want to convey the impression it left on me, for therein lies the true beauty.

Ram Dass famously said, "When you know how to listen, everybody is the guru." As we journey through life, we all search for answers. Most

believe these answers lie outside ourselves. I hope this book has encour-
aged you to share your authentic message with the world and look within
for solutions to your persistent questions. My sincere desire is that you
can overcome whatever has held you back from becoming the guru you
were born to be. What Baba Ji's response showed me was that we are all
gurus. No exceptions.

As I reflect on the Guru's Journey, both my own and the one you're
about to begin, I'm reminded that this path is ultimately about awakening to who you truly are. Every strategy in this book, every framework
and tactic, is simply a tool to help you remember your own inherent wisdom and share it with the world. Few people realize that others show up
in our lives to teach us lessons. Trauma, heartbreak, and struggle can be
disguised friends on our path to greatness. I believe Ram Dass empha-
sizes the value of humility, openness, and learning from others.

His quote reminds us that wisdom can come from anyone if we listen
deeply. This skill is crucial as you level up the Guru Ladder, because thought
leadership requires openness to continuous learning and growth. As you
move through the Six Phases of Mastery, you'll encounter new approaches
and people to learn from. Even as a guru, you must remain receptive to
wisdom from all sources. There's always something new to learn in your
field, and maintaining an open mind is central to a guru's personal credo.
This helps avoid the traps of ego and arrogance as your influence grows.
Remembering that everyone is a guru will help you authentically listen to
others and renew your commitment to serving them.

Often, we succeed, then stop when circumstances change or become
difficult. Fortunately, there will always be other gurus playing various
roles for you to learn from as you navigate life's journey. Like with the
Guru Ladder, we must keep climbing, even facing adversity. Then, you
prove to yourself that your future is truly limitless.

As promised, here's the amazing quote from Baba Ji himself. Let
his beautiful words close my book. The more you view creativity as a

limitless pathway to discovering new adventures, friends, and opportunities, the easier your journey to becoming a guru will be. Allow yourself to learn the lessons others in your life are trying to teach you. When everyone is a guru, your ego diminishes just enough to allow you to serve selflessly, live fearlessly, and lead thoughtfully. Baba Ji's quote reminds us that unity is the path all gurus seek, because inside each of us is a guru trying to speak—all we need to do is be quiet and still enough to listen.

"Imagine the sun shining brightly in the sky. Each ray of sunlight reaches out and touches the Earth, illuminating it in countless unique ways. These rays are like the many types of people in the world, each with their own path and purpose, shining their light in different directions. However, just as these rays originate from the same sun, all people are ultimately connected to a singular Source. When a soul passes away, it's like a sunbeam returning to its origin. Each individual ray may seem distinct, but they all merge back into the unity of the sun, just as souls return to the greater whole from which they came."

As I sat there, absorbing Baba Ji's words, I felt a shift within me—a quiet unraveling of something I hadn't realized I'd been clinging to. His metaphor of the sun and its rays echoed in my mind, and I thought back to the question I had posed at the beginning of this journey: *What if life is just a dream, and when you die, you wake up?*

Baba Ji's wisdom offered an answer not as a definitive truth but as an invitation to see beyond the layers of identity we construct. The ego, the version of ourselves built through experiences, fears, and desires, is like a single ray of sunlight. It shines brightly, convinced of its separateness and individuality. But when that ray returns to the sun, it doesn't disappear—it merges. It becomes part of something greater, something infinite.

Similarly, when the ego dies, when the version of ourselves we've fought to protect finally dissolves, we don't cease to exist. We awaken. We return to the Source, to the unity that has always been there, waiting beneath the surface of our constructed selves. This awakening isn't an end; it's a homecoming. It's the moment we realize that the dream of separation was just that: a dream. And in waking up, we find we were never truly apart from the whole.

This is the final awakening: realizing that the "you" you've feared losing was never the real you. The real you is the sun, not the ray. The real you is the ocean, not the wave. And when the wave crashes upon the shore, it doesn't disappear. It simply returns to the vastness from which it came.

So, as you close this book and continue your journey, remember: The ego's death is not something to fear. It is the doorway to awakening. It is the moment you shed layers of illusion and step into the truth of who you are. And when you do, you'll find that the dream of life was never meant to trap you, it was meant to lead you back to yourself.

Baba Ji's words linger in the air, a gentle reminder that we are all rays of the same sun, all waves in the same ocean. And as the crowd slowly rises, their faces softened by the weight of his wisdom, I feel it, too, the quiet pull of unity, the promise of awakening.

The dream is beautiful, but the awakening is even more beautiful.

ACKNOWLEDGMENTS

Writing this book has been a journey that wouldn't have been possible without the incredible people who shaped my path and supported me along the way.

Mom and Dad

Mummy and Daddy

Pamela Garrett

Roy Cammarano

Jason Chauhan

Joshua Ticsay

The Mike Ferry Family

Sanjay Chauhan

Neil Patel

Sujan Patel

Neil Schwartz

To everyone who contributed to this journey, whether through a conversation, a challenge, or simply by being part of my story—thank you. This book exists because of all of you.

NOTES

1. Dan Schawbel, "Building a Career Is About Flexibility, Curiosity and Adaptability," *Forbes*, September 13, 2016, https://www.forbes.com/sites/danschawbel/2016/09/13/neil-patel-building-a-career-is-about-flexibility-curiosity-and-adaptability/.
2. "'Wisdom' vs. 'Knowledge': What's the Difference?" August 23, 2022, *Dictionary.com*, https://www.dictionary.com/e/wisdom-vs-knowledge/.
3. Steve Jobs, "'You've Got to Find What You Love,' Jobs says," *Stanford Report*, June 12, 2005, https://news.stanford.edu/stories/2005/06/youve-got-find-love-jobs-says.
4. Henry David Thoreau, *The Writings of Henry David Thoreau: Journal, Volume II* (Riverside Press, 1906), 373, https://www.walden.org/wp-content/uploads/2016/02/Journal-2-Chapter-7.pdf.
5. Gene Weingarten, "Pearls Before Breakfast: Can One of the Nation's Great Musicians Cut Through the Fog of a D.C. Rush Hour? Let's Find Out," *Washington Post*, April 8, 2007, https://www.washingtonpost.com/lifestyle/magazine/pearls-before-breakfast-can-one-of-the-nations-great-musicians-cut-through-the-fog-of-a-dc-rush-hour-lets-find-out/2014/09/23/8a6d46da-4331-11e4-b47c-f5889e061e5f_story.html.
6. Alex Hormozi, (@AlexHormozi), "Entrepreneurship isn't a game of best man wins. It's a game of last man standing," Twitter (X), July 14, 2024, https://x.com/AlexHormozi/status/1812455799832170835.

7. Stacy Jo Dixon, "Daily Time Spent on Social Networking by Internet Users Worldwide from 2012 to 2024," *Statista*, April 10, 2024, https://www.statista.com/statistics/433871/daily-social-media-usage -worldwide/.

8. William Bruce Cameron, *Informal Sociology: A Casual Introduction to Sociological Thinking* (Random House, 1963): 4, accessed online July 29, 2025, https://archive.org/details/informalsociolog0000came/page /4/mode/1up?q=everything+that+counts.

9. Jesse Yomtov, "How Much Does a Super Bowl Commercial Cost in 2025? 30-Second Ads Hit New Heights," *Ad Meter*, January 29, 2025, https:// admeter.usatoday.com/story/sports/ad-meter/2025/01/29/super-bowl -commercial-cost-history/78032191007/.

10. "The Creator Economy Could Approach Half-a-Trillion Dollars by 2027," Goldman Sachs, April 19, 2023, https://www.goldmansachs .com/insights/articles/the-creator-economy-could-approach-half -a-trillion-dollars-by-2027.

11. Leon C. Megginson, "Lessons from Europe for American Business," *Southwestern Social Science Quarterly* 44, no. 1 (1963): 4. See also "The Evolution of a Misquotation," Darwin Correspondence Project, University of Cambridge, accessed July 29, 2025, https://www .darwinproject.ac.uk/people/about-darwin/six-things-darwin-never -said/evolution-misquotation.

12. Robin Geuens, "What is the average time spent on social media each day?" *Soax*, May 20, 2025, https://soax.com/research/time-spent-on -social-media.

ABOUT THE AUTHOR

AJ KUMAR is a digital marketing expert and founder of The Limitless Company, a social media innovation studio that transforms founders, CEOs, and subject matter experts into powerful personal media brands. Known as the "Digital Maestro," AJ helps creators and entrepreneurs build personality-driven media companies that convert attention into real business growth.

His journey began in high school, where he connected with renowned marketer Neil Patel. This early mentorship sparked a deep interest in digital strategy. AJ later sharpened his skills at a San Francisco agency, but his true breakthrough came while working with author Kimberly Snyder. Under AJ's guidance, Kimberly's brand exploded—drawing over 500,000 monthly blog readers, generating millions in revenue, and earning multiple *New York Times* bestsellers.

In 2020, AJ launched The Limitless Company to scale his success formula. His agency specializes in helping experts define their unique brand identity, produce compelling social-first content, and distribute it strategically across platforms. AJ's method blends creativity with performance, using data to transform attention into lasting business value.

AJ's mission is to amplify expert voices that deserve to be heard. He believes the right ideas shared by the right people can create meaningful change. Through The Limitless Company, AJ helps experts build the platforms and systems they need to turn their expertise into influence and impact.

**Don't Just Read GURU, INC. —
Live It.**

Unlock exclusive reader-only
bonuses:

- The Guru Inc. Workbook
- Blueprints & Guides
- Free Courses
- Advanced Trainings
- And more!

Access it all at
www.ajkumar.com/book

For consulting or private advising,
contact AJ directly: aj@ajkumar.com